G000154544

Although I already   up the
book, I was so captivated by it that I couldn't put it down until
I'd finished it. A wonderful, moving account of her profound
experience of looking death in the face and finding that God
can meet you there and do a phenomenal life-transforming
miracle. Your life will be enriched through reading it.

*Terry Virgo is the founder of Newfrontiers. He is a well-known
international Bible teacher and author and is based at
The King's Church, Burgess Hill, West Sussex.*

Swallowed by Life is a truly remarkable story – a story of faith
defeating fear, of hope defeating despair, of trust defeating
anxiety and of God's power defeating terminal illness. As
the story unfolds, we're taken through a range of emotions
– from the depths of despair to triumphant victory – and we
encounter the reality of someone clinging to God. Pathos
and humour combine to help us understand the working of
a loving heavenly Father as he preserves the life of one of
his precious children. This is a journey shared by a group
of loving friends who faithfully prayed and refused to give
in. When a hospital consultant recognises that persevering
prayer is the only explanation for a miraculous healing, then
God is clearly at work. In more than forty years of Christian
ministry I've seen many healing miracles but this one stands
out as one of the most extraordinary. *Swallowed by Life* inspires
faith, perseverance and confidence in a mighty God who's
concerned with every detail of life. He still heals today and
this astonishing story demonstrates this wonderful truth.

*David Fellingham is a renowned Bible teacher, songwriter and
author. He is based at King's Church, Horsham, West Sussex.*

I have loved reading this book which relates a remarkable journey through cancer with life coming out victorious. It is a very honest story filled with the human realities that come with the diagnosis and treatment of cancer. But not only that, it is also a reliable account of Christian faith in the goodness and power of God.

As a medical doctor I am delighted to help people with the resources at my disposal, but as a Christian I also have the heavenly resources available because of Jesus. I deeply appreciate the combination of excellent physical care and the loving power of God working together to bring health. This story shows that combination coming together in an amazing and beautiful way.

Over the course of many years I have been privileged to see people restored to life in numerous different ways and have heard many accounts of God's miraculous intervention working alongside great medical care. These reports stimulate our faith – and Liz's story certainly counts among them. I am delighted that such stories are becoming more common as Christians learn to access the love and power of God in very real ways, just as Liz relates in this book.

I am sure you will be moved and encouraged as you read her wonderful story.

Dr Pete Carter MBChB
Medical General Practitioner in Kent, Founder and
Director of the Eastgate Healing Centre
(www.eastgate.org.uk) and author of Unwrapping Lazarus.

Stories like this don't come along very often. At times I can be as sceptical as anyone, but I know Liz and had the privilege of seeing her remarkable journey from pretty close up. For me, the most miraculous part of the story was probably seeing God take her from a very dark place of fear to a point where she was much more peaceful about the prospect of dying. Astonishingly, she didn't die! She just got stronger and stronger. It wasn't possible to pinpoint a precise moment, heroic person or prayer that did the job. Rather, it simply seemed to be the power of Jesus at work in and through his worldwide community, the church. This puts the ultimate focus where it should be – to quote the famous hymn: To God be the glory, great things **HE** has done.

Steve Walford, Church Elder, Church of Christ the King, Brighton.

SWALLOWED
BY LIFE

'While we live in this earthly tent we groan with a feeling of oppression; it is not that we want to get rid of our earthly body, but that we want to have the heavenly one put on over us, so that what is mortal will be swallowed up by life'

2 Corinthians 5: 4, Good News Bible

SWALLOWED BY LIFE

Liz Woodgate with Mary Austin

New Wine Press

Published by New Wine Press
An imprint of RoperPenberthy Publishing Ltd,
19 Egerton Place, Weybridge,
Surrey KT13 0PF

DISCLAIMER
The names of certain people have been changed to
protect their identity.

ISBN 978 1 910848 12 8

Cover design by Esther Kotecha
Typeset in 10.5pt Palatino
by Avocet Typeset, Somerton, Somerset TA11 6RT
Printed in United Kingdom

SPECIAL THANKS

So many people played a part in my story. It was as though a great composer had chosen each one individually and put them together to form an orchestra. At his direction, they came in on cue: some having significant roles, others filling in now and again, everyone equally important. And maybe after reading this book you'll be able to decide for yourself whether the One behind it all should receive the standing ovation that I believe he deserves.

So thank you to:

My family: Mum, Sue & Mike, Jane & Alan, Hannah, Sarah (SP), James, Matt, Jonny, Tim, David, Peter & Ben, Sarah, Andy & Russell

Sussex Central YMCA: David & Vanessa, friends and colleagues

Church of Christ the King, Brighton: Steve & Rosey; Ken, Aafje & family

the Monday prayer group: Valerie, Claire, Irene, Tracy, Julie, (Sue)

Christine, Pauline and the congregation and friends at Church of Christ the King, Brighton

Other churches: Chrissie (City Coast Church, Brighton), Jan (Southwick Methodist), Angela (St Peters, Brighton), Will (The Point, Burgess Hill), Dave (Kings Church, Horsham), friends at Church of the Good Shepherd, Brighton, friends at Ruach Church, Lindfield

Royal Sussex County Hospital: Consultants & medical staff, Digestive Diseases Department; Dr Robinson, Consultant in Clinical Oncology, Sussex Cancer Centre

Hospital MacMillan Nurses

Hove Medical Centre: my GP – Dr A Mahony

Hove Polyclinic

Martlets Hospice, Hove: Day Centre Staff – Julie, Gordon, Caroline, Kay; volunteers – Brian, Owen, Sally & Sandra, MacMillan Community Team – Sheila & Mary

Friends from Auckland, New Zealand: Craig & Jenni Marsh

CONTENTS

FOREWORD

Right from the start I'd like to say that Liz is real! This true, often humorous, story will so encourage you. As you read you'll find yourself on a journey with her, watching the way she handled the conundrum when things seemed to be getting worse and God appeared not to be listening. You'll hear about her struggles with depression and despair and discover that God had a plan for her and never leaves it too late. You'll realise too how much she owed to the people who supported her, many of whom tenaciously clung to God's promises and refused to stop praying. God responded to their persistent faith in a remarkable, even unbelievable way.

There's a dynamic concerning God's intervention. Some people refer to the Greek word for 'time' and call it a 'Kairos' moment – a special designated moment when God chooses to move. I flew from New Zealand to England sensing that he was going to do something special. I wasn't disappointed. I'll never forget that awesome occasion. Immediately we started praying for Liz it was as though God flicked a switch and sealed a stunning healing miracle.

So be encouraged. God hears the cry of your heart and will respond to you in his time. Never be tempted to give up. Who knows what he'll do for you?

Craig Marsh
Turning Point Ministries, New Zealand.

CHAPTER 1

FREEFALL

Monday 27 September 2010 was a clear, sunny day and I was gazing through the window towards the sea. This was not a particularly noteworthy activity. Lots of people like looking out of windows at nice scenes. But this window was in a Consultant Surgeon's office on the ninth floor of the Millennium Wing of the Royal Sussex County Hospital in Brighton. Outside the view was great; inside I was in freefall. Just six months earlier I'd begun to have trouble digesting food. Even a colleague at work had commented, 'Have you noticed that every time you eat you have a coughing episode?' Initially I put it down to indigestion or reflux but from April I began to experience other problems. I lost weight and had pains in my central right side radiating to my back. The effect of all this was devastating. Ever since my late teens I'd grappled with bouts of debilitating anxiety and clinical depression and the prospect of having my life defined by them was overwhelming. I was forty-three years old and as I grew older my ability to bounce back was waning. I descended into a cycle of chronic anxiety which would later spiral downward into a deep depression. Sleep evaded me and a sense of foreboding plagued my mind. By June I was finding it hard to keep things together at my PA job at Sussex Central YMCA (formerly Hove YMCA). My boss noted my distress and was very kind to me, suggesting that I sign myself off sick for a while. So I went to my GP and he handed me a certificate for two weeks' break from work and a prescription for anti-depressants. I'd battled to avoid the anti-depressant route, but was forced to give in. 'It will just be for a short while,' I thought. 'Soon I'll be off the medication and feeling much better. I'll be back in the office in no time.' Little did I realise then how permanent that signing off would actually be.

My physical condition deteriorated even further and I was overcome by an extreme, highly unusual tiredness. I was so weary that I couldn't even do basic gardening and had to drag a chair outside so that I could stop periodically and rest. I tried to do brisk walks around the block but by the time I got home I was absolutely exhausted. My appetite was almost nil and when I did eat, I experienced a gurgling noise which carried on for an hour or so. It was horrible. I sounded like a partially-blocked drain! My severe problems forced me to move out of my house and into Mum's. One day I was eating a chicken salad in the kitchen and a piece of meat got stuck in my gullet. It just wouldn't shift. I moved round the house thinking that being upright would help to alleviate the problem, but I finally ended up on my knees, bent forward, struggling and panicking and trying to get the food up or down or something. I desperately wanted to alert Mum to phone for an ambulance, but I couldn't speak, so I resorted to frantic hand gestures. In the fifteen minutes or so the ambulance took to arrive, the meat slowly became dislodged and I avoided a trip to A&E.

By this time I was regularly visiting my GP who assumed that my main problems were mental and emotional. It never really occurred to either of us that the central issue wasn't depression at all. My emotional state was simply masking something far worse which was rumbling on unaddressed. On 18 July I went with Mum to a family celebration. The son of my sister, Jane, was having his fourth birthday party. I didn't feel well from the start, possibly because my GP had recently prescribed a drug to empty my stomach faster. When I arrived at Jane's house I was sick several times. There was blood in my vomit and when Mum and I returned home I got out of the car and nearly collapsed on the pavement. I was in a very bad way. The anxiety and depression weren't improving and for my own good I was sleeping on a mattress at the foot of Mum's bed. Lying down seemed to make my symptoms worse and I was experiencing regular and severe night sweats. My digestive system would gurgle incessantly and my anxiety would reach new heights. In desperation I approached my GP again. 'Something really isn't right,' I told him. 'I feel out of kilter. I've got to know what's wrong with me. Please could you arrange for me to have some tests?' He consented to my request and referred me to the Digestive Diseases Department at the Sussex County Hospital and also to Hove Polyclinic where I could receive counselling from mental health nurses in an attempt to get to the bottom of my anxiety state. On 24 August I went to the hospital to see a man with the impressive title of 'consultant, acute physician and gastroenterologist'! After examining me he wrote to my GP to confirm what I'd told him, namely: food was sticking for about two minutes in the lower part of my oesophagus; I was occasionally vomiting; I was losing weight; I had intermittent pain in my lumbar spine and right arm; I was coughing after meals and I was suffering from acute anxiety. He wasn't particularly alarmed at my condition and suspected nothing sinister. Rather he thought that there was probably a 'functional cause' like a mild hiatus hernia. However, just to be on the safe side, he arranged for me to have a barium swallow on 7 September to discover what was going on.

Two days after that procedure my GP phoned me at home very concerned and asked me to attend the surgery the following day. When I sat down with him he told me, 'They've found something in the test that they didn't expect to see. You have an appointment for a gastroscopy on 13 September.' Suddenly, things started moving very fast. I had the gastroscopy. The medical staff inserted a long flexible tube down my food pipe into my stomach. It had a light and a video camera at its end and they were able to see on a television screen exactly what was happening inside me. They also took a biopsy – a small sample of tissue which they could examine with a microscope. I was also informed that I'd need a CT scan. The consultant who performed the gastroscopy suggested that I should go on a soft diet. He didn't realise that after the chicken salad incident and subsequent swallowing difficulties, I was already adjusting my eating habits. 'Would you like to see the gastroscopy pictures?' asked a male nurse after the examination. 'Yes,' I replied, and he pointed to an area in the picture and said, 'At least half of your oesophagus is blocked by that lump. You'll need to get it removed or you'll really have difficulty swallowing anything within the next few weeks.' I must have responded in a very matter of fact way because he added, 'You're very calm'. What he didn't realise was that although my mind was receiving the information, my heart remained oblivious to the life threatening implications of what he was saying. On 21 September I had the CT scan because the specialists wanted a more comprehensive view of what was going on inside my chest and thorax.

Everything was happening at once! The following day I was at Hove Polyclinic having my initial one-to-one meeting with a mental health nurse who was trying to manage my acute anxiety. One of the relaxation techniques that they suggested was for me to lie flat, listen to music and concentrate intensely on the lyrics and my breathing. So I'd often stretch out on the lounge floor and play *Skyline Pigeon*, one of my favourite Elton John songs, over and over again.

A week after my CT scan I returned to the hospital for an appointment with Mr Hale, the Consultant Surgeon, who was going to update me on the results of the investigations. Mum and Sue (who was an experienced staff nurse), went with me and we had to wait for quite a while because there was an emergency in another part of the hospital which Mr Hale had to attend urgently. I looked round at the people in the waiting room. Many were elderly and among them was Georgie, an ex-work colleague who was accompanying her Dad. I sat next to her and chatted. 'Is this appointment for your Mum?' she asked. 'No,' I replied, 'it's for me.' She looked quite surprised.

Was I worried? Actually, not really – because I couldn't register the seriousness of my situation. I just expected the casual comment, 'We've discovered a benign lump in your oesophagus but the good news is that we can remove it. So we've scheduled you in for surgery on such and such a date.' I couldn't have been more wrong. A nurse came over to us and called me into Mr Hale's consulting room. I sat down and he immediately asked me, 'Have you got anyone with you today?' 'Yes,' I replied, 'my Mum and sister are in the waiting room.' 'Then you need to get them,' he continued. 'They should be with you when I tell you what's going on.' As I walked out of his office I passed Georgie who was, by then, in the corridor. Noticing the concern on my face she asked, 'Is everything OK?' 'No,' I replied, 'I don't think it is.' I called Mum and Sue and we walked to Mr Hale's office together. We were joined by a nurse who sat quietly nearby. Mr Hale looked at me with a serious face. 'I have bad news for you,' he said. 'You've got cancer in your oesophagus. But we're going for a cure. Intensive chemotherapy should reduce the size of the tumour but you'll also require surgery to remove it. Meanwhile we'll need to do some more tests to ensure that the tumour hasn't spread.' Then, introducing the nurse, he said, 'This is Veronica. She's a Macmillan nurse and she's been assigned to support you.'

I looked over his shoulder at the view through the window. It really was glorious – a wide panorama of sparkling sea and cloudless blue sky. What I was hearing just didn't seem appropriate for such a beautiful day. Almost numb with shock I kept thinking: 'Cancer? It can't be. This kind of thing happens to others, not to me.' Sue sat there quietly. Mr Hale was simply confirming what she'd already suspected. Mum, on the other hand, seized on perhaps the only positive element in the entire scenario. 'Liz has a faith', she declared, 'she's a Christian.' As we left Mr Hale's office he put his hand on my shoulder, picked up on Mum's comment and said, 'If ever there were a time to start praying, it's now.'

CHAPTER 2

HAPPY DAYS

'The rabbit's got out again and the cat's chasing it around the garden.' Mum's shout up the stairs was designed to propel my sister, Jane and me into action. It was a fairly frequent event which usually occurred just before we went off to school. At Mum's cry we'd charge into the garden and leap around shouting instructions to one another. Our tactics involved securing the rabbit in a corner and chasing the cat in the opposite direction. After a few hectic minutes, we'd emerge with our arms wrapped round our two furry foes with looks of triumph on our faces. Happily, we always succeeded in our rescue missions.

Here's another window – the kitchen one. If, like Mum, you'd been looking through it, you'd have seen not just a couple of youngsters gallivanting round the garden, but also a sort of cameo of my early life. There were two elements: challenges, particularly in the early years, and vast amounts of pure fun. We were a lively mix of parents, daughters, pets, friends, activities, hobbies and games. I couldn't have wished for a better beginning.

It all started when Mum and Dad met. Dad came from a working class family. In his teens he joined a 'high' Anglican church and became a choir boy. At the end of World War 2, after serving in the army of occupation in Palestine and Italy, he studied hard, by correspondence course, to qualify as a certified accountant. Mum, an only child, was a day pupil at a convent school. In her late teens she became quite lonely and asked God for a husband. Within a short time she'd met Dad on a blind date. They were engaged two weeks' later but waited for a couple of years before they were married in 1959. Sue was born in 1960. Sue's arrival gave rise to one of the challenges. After her birth Mum suffered a severe hormone imbalance which tipped her into a psychotic state. As a result she and Sue were separated for several months. Dad struggled to visit his wife and child in different locations and also to hold down his full time job. The outcome could have been extremely serious had Mum not suddenly snapped out of it. She always viewed this turning point as a mini miracle.

There were two other 'birth oriented' events in my family which would have been picked up far earlier in a modern day maternity ward than they were then: the arrival of Jane and then me. In a nutshell, Mum and Dad had incompatible blood groups meaning that when Jane was born in 1963 she was acutely anaemic and had to be given large amounts of iron supplements. Four years later my birth was even more precarious because I was a rhesus negative baby. The antibodies in Mum's blood viewed me as a foreign body and attacked me in the womb with the result that I almost died.

During the last month of Mum's pregnancy I stopped moving. And when I was born Mum was told that I probably wouldn't last the night. The hospital staff whisked me away and I survived only because a visiting doctor knew that I needed a blood transfusion and had the expertise on how to do it. Once he'd saved my life I made a rapid recovery. My parents christened me Elizabeth, probably unaware that it meant 'my God is an oath'. In other words, 'my God is the absolutely faithful one.' I never appreciated quite how significant my name would become.

'Fidelity' was the word engraved round the inside of Mum's wedding ring. And faithfulness characterised their marriage. Dad was fiercely honest and hated anything crude. He was always on the side of the underdog and when his accountancy partnership disbanded he branched off alone with Mum typing up the accounts. If a client couldn't afford his fees, Dad would undercharge him and if he ever saw a need, he'd do his best to meet it. Money had no real hold over him. Rather, he was notorious for his generosity and at over-tipping people which sometimes irritated Mum. As I grew up I watched them, learnt from them and tried to adopt their values in my life.

The Woodgates enjoyed a happy, healthy and secure home together. We grew up in Hangleton and moved to Hove in 1976 when I was nine years old. They were happy times and full of life. I loved school and had a passion for music. I sang in the school choir and played the violin (or 'vile din' according to Jane) in the school orchestra! I also learnt the recorder, the piano and the trombone. I enjoyed playing chase, French skipping and marbles with my friends and joined the Brownies and the Guides. In my mid-teens I also had tennis lessons. There was a succession of pets: one white guinea pig (Snowy) who had about five babies, one tortoise (Fred), some fish in the pond (not named), one white rabbit (Penny) and one cat (Pussy Woodgate). The cat was a stray ginger Tom and was about six months' old. I found him when I was out roller skating with a friend and we both agreed that he needed a place to stay. Unfortunately, my friend's sister was allergic to cats. Pussy Woodgate landed on his paws in my home.

In March 1976 my Mum's mother died and Mum and Dad wanted to give a home to her husband, Freddie. That's the reason why in October 1976 we moved from the house in Hangleton to a larger property in Hove. Grandad Freddie lived with us for nearly a decade, to the ripe old age of ninety six. Grandad was a godly man who loved life. I used to spend hours in his room watching TV – together with the cat and a bag of sweets. He was a member of a local croquet club and I partnered him on a few occasions. He joined us on our family holidays to the Isle of Wight and Cornwall. He loved reading, listening to hymns and watching marching bands (having played the trombone in his younger days). He had a talent for writing short ditties to mark family events and I still have one that he composed for one of my birthdays.

Both Sue and Jane became Christians in 1978 while attending the youth group at the Church of the Good

Shepherd, Brighton. God didn't feature much in my life but I always believed in his existence and when my friends said that he wasn't real, I was quite shocked. 'Surely everyone knows there's a God,' I thought. Within the space of about two years I lost three of my grandparents; the death of my Dad's Mum being the most traumatic. One day he walked into her home and found her dead. This had a devastating effect on him and on me too – because there was a strong bond between us. He used to call me his 'little one'. With Grandma gone, I began feeling very vulnerable and fearful. Supposing Dad died? Where had my relatives gone? Where would I go when I died? Jane and I shared a bedroom. On Christmas Day 1978 she started explaining to me that it was possible to have a relationship with God, that he actually liked me and wanted to be my friend. To me this was exciting news. What did I need to do? Jane continued, 'It's not enough just to believe that he exists,' she said, 'You need to ask him to forgive you and to come into your life. Then you'll go to heaven when you die.' I wanted to be right with God so when she gave me a small Gideon Bible I told her that I'd pray the prayer on the back page – but later, when I was on my own.

As I'd promised, that night I prayed the prayer alone in the bedroom. I can't say that I had a dramatic experience of God, but over time I became aware of Him with me, together with a new sense of security and peace. Gradually my behaviour started to change; I stopped swearing and didn't descend so quickly into an angry rage when Jane beat me at board games! Even today I carry around that Gideon Bible in my handbag. On the last page, in my eleven year old handwriting, is the confirmation that on 25/12/78 Elizabeth Woodgate received Jesus Christ as her Saviour and Lord.

CHAPTER 3

SECRETS

So here I was, a bright-eyed, fun-filled eleven year old on the brink of a new life following Jesus. What exciting plans did he have in store for me? At that age I just lived one day at a time and enjoyed them all. No one would have guessed what lay just around the corner. Jesus was changing me and I was happy in my newfound faith – for the first eight months anyway. After that, the changes didn't seem quite so welcome.

The new Comprehensive school system began in September 1979 so I was among the first pupils to be involved in it. Hove Park Comprehensive was fine by me – except for the fact that my closest friends all parted company and went off to other schools. I felt lonely without them but developed a new friendship with a girl called Joy. And she was there when something happened that would devastate my life for years to come.

We were in the school canteen eating lunch together when I got some food stuck in my throat and had a bad choking fit. The episode left me shaken, but rather than tell my parents about it, I kept it to myself. On a superficial level it was just one of those things that happens which I naturally tried to forget about. But subconsciously, it started to dominate my thinking – with disastrous consequences. From that time on and into my early teens I began to dread eating in the company of others. Initially, I tried to avoid having lunch in the school canteen and if that didn't work, I'd nibble through tiny portions. I declined invitations to my friends' houses which naturally had the effect of isolating me. My fixation spilled over into my home life too. Before meals I'd often become anxious then I'd have a full blown panic attack. I became watchful of others when I was sitting at table with them. I had to give them the impression that everything was fine even when it wasn't – and I did a pretty good job of it. For a while, eating alone wasn't too much of a problem, but I gradually found even that difficult. My eating disorder became so bad that when I was about fifteen I used to creep downstairs in the night and force myself to consume half a piece of bread and drink a few sips of milk just to prove to myself that I could. No one ever heard me so my secret was safe. Indeed, I became an expert at hiding it and it became so much a part of me that I ended up believing that my behaviour was perfectly normal. I never really understood why the thought of eating created such terror. I wasn't suffering from anorexia because I was happy with the way I looked. If you'd asked me what the problem was I'd have said, 'I'm afraid of choking. It's up to me to sustain myself. If I can't manage my next meal I'll start to die.' A kind of hyper self-vigilance had set in. To any outsider, my behaviour was totally illogical, but to me it was all too real.

The days passed. I did well at church and at school. When I was about thirteen I was confirmed at the Church of the Good Shepherd and was involved with the youth group and Guides there. Four years later I joined Clarendon Church youth group which was called *Mustard Seed*, and went to the Downs Bible Week. In my late teens I was baptised in water and in the Holy Spirit and was regularly involved with the children's work at church.

At school, after gaining O and A Levels, I was ready to embark on my future career. My teachers encouraged me to go to university, but I knew that I wouldn't be able to cope with the study, living away from home and my severe eating disorder so I decided to follow my sisters into nursing. I enrolled locally at Southlands Hospital in Shoreham but left after just six months and took a job as a cashier/clerk at the Halifax Building Society in Brighton. Office work actually suited me much better than nursing but after eighteen months I realised that to progress further I'd need to be qualified in relevant skills such as typing, word processing and shorthand. So I began a secretarial course at Brighton Technical College. I did the two year course in one and loved it. By now I'd become used to leading a kind of double life. My closest friends knew my difficulties, but I managed to fool everyone else into thinking that I was perfectly OK. Somehow I was employing covert coping mechanisms and just about holding it together.

One Sunday afternoon in early October 1987 I was walking home from the house of some Christian friends when God seemed to speak to me. 'You must honour your parents and let them know what's going on,' he said. When I got home I found that Mum was out and Dad was watching football on the television. 'Dad,' I said, 'I've got something to tell you. It's serious.' And with that I switched off the TV, which really got his attention. I then explained all about my fears concerning food. Mum returned about thirty minutes later and I told her the truth too. They were naturally shocked and upset that I'd said nothing to them before.

Later that month the Great Storm hit the south coast. It reached hurricane proportions and marked a crescendo moment for my first breakdown. Anxiety and depression howled into my life and sleepless nights followed. Mum and Dad insisted that I see the GP who prescribed a cocktail of anti-depressants, beta blockers and sleeping pills. He couldn't understand the root of the problem. On one occasion he told me that I had the most unusual and irrational phobia that he'd ever seen in his entire career. He weighed me and, in great detail explained that I'd have to stop eating for over forty days before putting my life in danger. At this point the church leadership introduced me to a Christian psychologist who counselled me for a couple of years.

In June 1988, at the age of twenty-one, I attained my London Chamber of Commerce Private Secretary's Certificate along with other secretarial qualifications. The following month I secured a job as a clerk/typist with a company of consulting engineers in Brighton. I remained there for the next seventeen years, being promoted to departmental secretary and then PA to the Managing Director. I really enjoyed it. I had two further stress-related breakdowns: one when I was about twenty-three and the other four years later. On both occasions I was forced to return to the pills and to take several weeks' sick leave. Interestingly my GP noticed that once I started to pull out of the anxiety/depression I tended to improve very quickly indeed.

At this stage of life most young people would have been enjoying holidays with friends and perhaps considering marriage and children. But such was my emotional state that I couldn't cope with vacations or boyfriends. My dietary phobias were so overwhelming that I'd fail on both counts. So I focused on my work and on my church activities and spent quality time with my family and friends. I also bought a house in Hove and shared it with a succession of lodgers.

In 1995 when I was twenty-eight, Dad's health began to deteriorate. He had a form of dementia but Mum managed to keep him at home with her as long as possible, and I did my best to help. The next six years were demanding, but I managed to hold down my job and battle on. Then a crisis event on New Year's Day 2000 threatened to send me over the edge. We were at the kitchen table eating lunch when a piece of meat got stuck in Mum's throat and she began to choke. Dad would normally have reacted fast but he could no longer do much because of his advanced illness. 'Mum is going to die in front of me,' I thought. Panic-stricken, I dialled 999. After a couple of long minutes the meat shot out of Mum's mouth and the paramedics who arrived shortly afterwards found themselves surplus to requirements. It was a traumatising start to the millennium. Twenty days later my dear Dad was sectioned. He died in April 2001.

Three months after Dad's death I had a major breakdown and was off work for about twelve weeks. I felt as though I'd been hit by a freight train. I could hardly eat or sleep and my weight plummeted to seven and a half stone (50 kilos). I suffered from severe breathing difficulties and the adrenalin in my system caused me to jerk uncontrollably at night. Sleeping pills did nothing for me; after half an hour, I was wide awake and watching the hands of the clock go round and round till morning. I was totally exhausted by lack of sleep and my mind was spinning uncontrollably. It felt as though I'd fallen into a deep black well. I moved back in with Mum and began seeing Irene, a qualified and experienced counsellor from church. At that time there seemed to be a society-wide stigma over depression. I felt that this stigma also extended into some Christian circles where believers were frowned upon for apparently trusting their anti-depressants rather than God. For this reason I always tried to look as if I was getting on fine – until I couldn't do that any longer. Now I started speaking openly to my colleagues about my depression and anxiety and found that many of them responded well to me. They seemed to warm to the idea that Christians hadn't got it all together but had problems too, I found that some wanted to talk to me about their own difficulties. I edged my way back to work gradually and by November I was full time again.

My Managing Director retired in 2002 and in 2005 I decided to move on. I did some temping work notably as a secretary to a psychiatrist at The Dene Hospital, a medium secure unit for women in the prison system. Then I saw an advertisement in the local newspaper for a position as PA to the Chief Executive of the Hove YMCA. It was my dream job and I loved the charity aspect to it. I started in March 2007 three days before my fortieth birthday and walked out just over three years' later, unaware that I'd never return.

It was now July 2010. I fully expected to return to the office within two or three weeks and was trying my hardest to get fit again. With this in mind, Vanessa, the HR manager and member of my church, arranged an appointment with me to discuss how I might be able to ease myself back into work. Christians believe that God speaks to them and answers prayer. We hear his voice in all kinds of ways, for example through the Bible, circumstances, mental impressions and pictures. With this in mind, and when we'd finished our coffee, Vanessa and I decided to pray together for a couple of minutes. Then she surprised me by telling me that God had given her a picture for me. 'You were at the bottom of a mountain,' she said. 'There was a heavy mist everywhere and you could see only what was right in front of you. You had all sorts of climbing equipment – boots, pickaxe – everything you needed for the ascent, but you had to take one step at a time. Once you got to the summit you were way above the clouds and had a 360 degree view into a clear blue sky. I believe that God is saying that he's in control. There's a climb ahead but when you get to the top you'll understand why you had to take that route and what he's done for you.'

As I walked home I considered what she'd said. The idea of a demanding climb was quite daunting – hiking boots and thick mist suggested effort – but hadn't I already been through that? Surely I was now near the summit. God was comforting me and telling me that I'd soon be back at work, enjoying my job, with the depression far below me. I clung to this hope. It was the only encouragement that I received from God for the next five months – and that felt like a very long time.

CHAPTER 4

BAD NEWS

Mum, Sue and I left Mr Hale's consulting room and walked out of the hospital. We got into a waiting taxi and sat in shocked silence as the driver took us home. I remember gazing out of the window as the world passed by. People were crossing roads, meeting their friends, walking in the sun, sending texts, shopping and riding their bikes. And I had cancer. I wondered what the taxi driver thought of his uncommunicative passengers, but he said nothing to us. He deposited us outside the house and we went indoors. It was a strange homecoming. I was walking into familiar, but somehow foreign, territory. I felt as though I was in a parallel universe, on the outside looking in.

The numbness made it impossible for me to cry. Instead I went into mechanical mode and started thinking of the people that I needed to phone. My sister, Jane, was first on the list. Unlike Sue, she never suspected that I was so ill. My colleagues were just as devastated as she was. They knew that I was stressed but were expecting me to return to work within a short time. My friends, church leaders and other family members reacted with similar disbelief. At some point Mum went over to the kitchen calendar and in the space beside Monday 27 September 2010, wrote two words: 'Bad news.' Jane visited the following day and brought her son, Ben who was about nine months old. I watched my nephew wriggling on the floor and wondered 'Will I live to see him grow up?' Over the next few days several friends called round offering encouragement. I desperately needed their support.

It seemed ironic, inconceivable almost, that of all the problems I could have faced, God had permitted one related to eating. It was my worst fear and it had risen up to confront me. Inside my head a mocking voice kept challenging me: 'OK, Liz, get yourself out of this one.' I'd always been able to drive myself through difficulties but now I had no control. I couldn't win against cancer. Mum was right. It was bad news. Veronica, the Macmillan nurse, had given me some literature on oesophageal cancer. The booklet told me about the disease but didn't comment on the prognosis. I discovered that this cancer was more usual in older people, particularly among those who had been heavy drinkers or smokers. I understood then why my GP had missed it. I fulfilled none of the criteria.

By now the tumour was growing and my oesophagus narrowing to the point where I was able to swallow only soft foods. Friends came round with homemade soup which had no meat or vegetable pieces. Other than that, I survived on things like rice pudding, soggy cornflakes, yoghurt, milk and drinkable foodstuffs which contained more 'drink' than 'stuff'!

The TV soon lost its appeal, with people airing their opinions and complaining of seemingly trivial things. So Mum and I started to go out for short evening walks instead. I didn't particularly want to see people in the daytime, so a stroll at about 8:00pm when it was dark was an ideal alternative. We usually went round Hove Recreation Ground which was often illuminated by the lights of the Hove Rugby Club. Mum and I would talk and I would ask her how was I going to cope with a death sentence. At last, the tears began to flow.

On 4 October I returned to the hospital with Mum to see Dr Davis, a consultant radiologist. He performed an endoscopic ultrasound, an examination of the lining of my gullet and into the stomach, to obtain a 3D image to determine the size and extent of the tumour. 'You could benefit from having a stent fitted,' he said. 'It would certainly improve your swallow.'

That afternoon Sue joined us and we saw a senior registrar who told us that the tumour was about seven centimetres in diameter. 'The cancer is at stage three to four,' he commented. I hadn't a clue what that meant and over the following weeks I did some research on the Internet to find out. Maybe that was a bad move. When I learnt what I was fighting, Internet browsing had the effect of fuelling my fear. I discovered that stage four was the final phase of cancer. I also read that oesophageal cancer was a brutal disease which some sufferers and their families called 'The Beast'. It had a low survival rate, its location made it hard to treat and many sufferers died within a year of diagnosis. Their stories unnerved me. Why had God allowed me to have this particular cancer? Why couldn't it have been something else?

The next step was a PET (Positron Emission Tomography) scan which would tell the doctors whether the cancer had spread to other parts of my body. If there were secondary growths, then nothing else could be done. If it was contained, then I could receive chemotherapy. The scan was scheduled for 5 October, but had to be postponed because I absent-mindedly ate a small piece of banana for breakfast! Another appointment was made for 11 October. On 6 October I received a visit from two of my church elders who talked to me and prayed. A couple of days later another friend, Angela popped round and started taking me for rides in her new car (a lovely Mini convertible). She prayed for me on several occasions and said one day, 'I think you could write a book at the end of all this.'

I had the PET scan at Brighton University and spent three agonizing days waiting for the results. On 14 October I sat down with Dr Robinson, the oncologist at the Sussex Cancer Centre. 'It hasn't spread,' he said, and I was so relieved that I became tearful. He examined me and said, 'You'll need intensive chemotherapy because the cancer is aggressive. You'll be taking two drugs over the next two months. We'll give you daily chemo tablets and three cycles of intravenous chemotherapy.' 'Will I lose my hair?' I asked. 'No, he replied. 'I did consider an additional drug which would have caused hair loss, but I've decided against it.' I welcomed this news. It was like a tiny ray of light in a pit of gloom.

The members of the small church home group that I attended struggled to come to terms with what was happening to me. But from the outset, Ken and Aafje, the leaders, rallied its members and other friends and prayed that God would perform a miracle for me. When they met together they often fasted, and they sent out regular e-mails with updates, Scriptures and encouragements to help everyone to know what to pray for.

On my second appointment at the Polyclinic, I sat down with two of the mental health nurses and told them that I had oesophageal cancer, that I was a Christian and that I was really scared. They were shocked into silence, probably thinking, 'Well, here's this woman suffering from anxiety and clinical depression and now she's got something to be anxious and depressed about! Where do we go from here? How on earth do we respond to what she's telling us?' I had only three or four appointments with them, then the cancer encroached on my life too much for me to continue attending.

The international story of the moment concerned the Chilean mining accident in a copper-gold mine, where, on 5 August, a cave-in trapped thirty-three miners 700 metres underground. It was thought that none of them could have survived the collapse, and if they had they'd probably have starved to death. But the miners prayed, as did many others around the world, and their rescuers made contact with them on 22 August. The following day they'd drilled a twelve centimetre wide borehole and were lowering supplies through it to the men. On 31 August the rescuers began drilling a shaft and on 17 September the drill broke through to the captives. When this hole was wide enough, the rescuers sent down a man in a purpose built tube to help with the rescue. On 13 October all the miners were brought to the surface.

With this story in mind, Sue got the very strong impression that God had a similar plan for me. I was at the bottom of a pit, totally unreachable. Not only was I seriously depressed; I now had cancer. It was a dark, desperate and hopeless situation, but people were praying and Sue sensed that God was telling her, 'I'm sending a man.'

The pain through my core and in my back was steadily increasing and I was finding it hard to eat or drink anything at all. In addition, I was continuing to suffer from panic attacks and depression and was periodically struggling to get through even one hour of the day. This made it difficult for my family or friends to get near to me. I was trying to draw on God, but remained largely isolated and close to desperation. By this time I was receiving regular visits from Steve, one of the church leaders, and from Irene, my church counsellor. The hospital Macmillan nurse was incredibly sympathetic towards me. She was my main point of contact with the specialists, and she was also a great listener so I was often on the phone to her.

The next hospital visit was on 21 October when I was due to see a nurse from the Cancer Centre to discuss the chemotherapy. When Mum and I walked into the room he assumed that Mum was the patient, which accentuated how unusual this cancer was in younger people. He told me that I might suffer with a lot of sickness as a result of the treatment. My reasoning was simple, 'If that's the case, what will I be sick with, and might I choke?' I was getting close to a point where I could consume little more than water and presumably any stomach contents would find it hard to get past the tumour up my oesophagus anyway!

My swallow was becoming critical and I'd read that the insertion of a stent was a medical intervention when swallowing became a serious problem. In fact, it was actually my last resort. At this time I was receiving a lot of support from the MacMillan community team based at the Martlets hospice. On two occasions one of the nurses visited me and I expressed my concerns to her over the stent. 'If it's fitted, what happens if it doesn't work? Maybe I'll starve to death.' She allayed my fears, drew diagrams to help me understand the procedure and really encouraged me. So I started pressing hard to have the stent. I phoned Dr Davis' secretary several times and succeeded in getting the operation scheduled for 28 October, the day before chemotherapy would begin.

Mum went with me to the Interventional Radiology

Department but stayed in the waiting room. Dr Davis' assistant spoke to me about the possible side effects and risks involved. 'The stent could work its way up or down your oesophagus with equally serious consequences' he said. 'If it migrates upwards it could choke you and if it moves downwards it could perforate your oesophagus and you could bleed to death.' 'What alternative do I have?' I replied. And with that I signed the consent form.

So what was this stent? I wondered if it was a kind of rigid pipe! Dr Davis cleared up that misconception by showing it to me. It had to hold back the tumour, so I'd say that it looked about ten centimetres in length and about a centimetre wide. It was a metal mesh tube which was reinforced with a metal band at each end. 'Will I be able to bend with this thing in?' I asked naively. He grinned and replied, 'Yes, you will. This is your flexible friend!'

I discovered that I'd be mildly sedated throughout the procedure. The tumour was spreading inwards from the wall of my lower oesophagus creating a smaller and smaller hole through which food and drink could pass. The goal would be to insert the stent through this hole. Once in position, it would expand over a period of about twenty four hours and push the tumour back, widening the oesophagus in the process. Then I should be able to eat and drink more normally. There was a kind of symmetry in all this: a borehole had been created for food to be lowered to the trapped Chilean miners. It kept them alive until the rescue day.

The staff prepped me for the small operation and Dr Davis began his work. He had difficulty getting the stent into position so he took his time and succeeded after several uncomfortable attempts. I was wheeled into the recovery room where I lay next to a woman who'd just had the same surgical procedure. She was about eighty years old. An information sheet told me what I could and couldn't eat – namely anything that could potentially get stuck. It warned me to chew everything really well and to have plenty of fizzy drinks before, during and especially after my meals. The carbon dioxide solution would help to keep the stent clean. I was advised to sit upright when

I ate so that gravity would do the job of getting food down into my stomach.

I went home and lay down on my bed. The stent had begun to expand and by midnight I was in considerable pain. But by the following morning I was feeling better and decided to make myself a mug of tea. Everything surrounding that hot liquid is etched into my memory! It was about 8:00am and the drink was made from a Sainsbury's Red Label teabag. I took it upstairs and instead of taking bird-like sips which gurgled their way through my gullet, I took huge gulps which went straight down inside me. It was fantastic – like nectar – the best mug of tea that I've ever drunk.

CHAPTER 5

CHEMOTHERAPY

With the tea still settling happily in my stomach, I was on my way back to the hospital Cancer Centre for my 10:30am Chemotherapy infusion. Mum was with me and the whole experience was pretty surreal. There I was, enjoying a short period of respite when things had gained a semblance of normality, and then being catapulted into something that was both uncomfortable and far from normal. Patients were sitting in bays around the room hooked up to intravenous drips. Some of them looked quite content. They were well into their reading material and were tucking into homemade sandwiches or hospital food. I wondered whether they were looking forward to a cooked meal when they got home. With others, it was more outwardly apparent that they were extremely ill and seemed incapable of looking a sandwich in the face, let alone eating it.

The doctors were giving me a fighting chance of beating the cancer and hoped that the treatment would slow it down and shrink the tumour. This first session lasted about three hours and while I sat there, the 'liquid poison' dripping steadily into my arm, I struck up a brief conversation with a woman in the bay opposite. She'd had a number of infusions and was able to calm me down. It was really helpful to talk to other patients both on this, and on my two subsequent visits to the Cancer Suite.

The nurse warned me that in the coming weeks I should avoid anything cold – not just food and drink but also cold weather and cold objects – because I might suffer some side effects with the particular chemotherapy drugs that I was on. I wish I'd listened more closely to that last piece of advice because in the final ten minutes of the infusion I took a tiny sip of chilled water and immediately regretted it. The cold drink sent my face and hands into spasm and I had to stay an extra hour while my body partially recovered. Unfortunately, the weather outside was particularly icy. A nurse wrapped my head, neck and upper body in a blanket, to wear until I got home but I couldn't avoid the cold air altogether and within about three hours I was again in trouble. My hands were curling up like arthritic claws and my toes were crossing. I lost all feeling down one side of my face and was finding it hard to talk. I looked as if I'd had a stroke and was afraid by what was happening to me. Mum and Sue were so shocked by my physical state that later that evening Sue was on the phone to a nurse on one of the Cancer Wards asking what we should do. 'Don't panic,' she said, 'this can happen.'

I found that I simply dared not make contact with anything remotely cold. That didn't just include cold food and drink, but things like cold cutlery and cold air too. Just breathing in the winter air would send my throat into spasm. If I went for a short walk with a scarf wrapped round by face I must have resembled Scott of the Antarctic. I couldn't walk across the kitchen lino without something on my feet and I had to clean my teeth in warm water. When Sue gave me a pair of fingerless gloves I wore them 24/7, but even then I suffered from constant tingling and numbness in my hands. I would have benefitted from a onesie, but they hadn't been invented then!

Within a couple of days I was due to take the daily oral medication. Four huge tablets had to be dissolved in about 500 millilitres of water and the mixture tasted dreadful. Any fit person would probably have downed the lot as fast as possible, but I battled to get any of it into me. Then the chronic sickness started. After five days I was on the phone to Dr Robinson. 'I can't do it. It's untenable. I feel awful and the tablets are making me feel so very sick.' 'OK,' he replied.

'We'll skip them until after the second infusion. Then I'll reduce the dose.' I breathed a sigh of relief.

The stent was a mixed blessing. It gave me a lifeline but I was all too aware of its physical presence inside me and that was incredibly disconcerting. Added to this, the stent was holding my oesophagus wide open which created problems because it restricted the muscle contractions of my gullet (peristalsis). I was reliant on gravity to make food go down which meant that I had to adopt a good posture whenever I ate or drank. Also, I was unable to lie flat at night as otherwise I'd be at risk of aspirating my stomach contents into my lungs, and possibly contracting pneumonia. To avoid this I had to sleep upright which wasn't exactly relaxing. I was supplied with an electric bed elevator which raised my upper body at night. It was a big help but didn't entirely solve the problem because there was no board at the bottom of my bed so I kept slipping down. I was becoming nervous whenever I ate anything, being convinced that it was becoming stuck in the stent. I was swallowing food downwards and vomiting it upwards, so could I know if the stent was coping?! I was soon on the phone to Veronica seeking reassurance and asking her if it could be removed. She tried hard to allay my fears. 'The stent is doing you good,' she reasoned. 'It's keeping you alive.'

I was told that once the chemotherapy had done its work, I'd need a major operation at the end of January. The surgery would involve the removal of the tumour (and stent) together with the affected section of my oesophagus. My stomach would then be pulled up and repositioned higher, with life-changing consequences. Veronica was clear about what I could expect. If the stent was hard to manage, it would be even more challenging to cope with a permanent and uncomfortable shift of my internal organs. I understood that following the operation I'd require two to three months' recovery time and that my future lifestyle would be almost unrecognisable. It would revolve totally around food. I'd need to have a balanced diet and instead of eating a good meal three times a day, my new stomach shape would enable me to eat only little portions and I would have to eat more frequently. If I went out with my friends I'd probably be able to manage only a slice of pizza and a small drink. At least I knew what was going to happen to me, but the prospect greatly distressed me. Veronica was on the receiving end of countless phone calls and she encouraged me to press through the next couple of months prior to the operation.

The second infusion was on 19 November. On this occasion I chatted to a couple of older men. One of them was on the same strict regime as me and we shared our experiences of negotiating cold kitchen floors, opening the fridge door and having ten seconds to grab something, and of being robbed of the chance of a midnight feast! We laughed a lot – it was great medicine. I also managed to eat a Kit Kat and a yogurt.

I left the hospital with vast quantities of chemo tablets and suspensions which we put in Mum's bedroom. We joked that there were so many bottles that it looked just like a chemist's shop. The new chemotherapy tablets were small so they didn't have to be dissolved as before, but could be swallowed with a glass of water. I was to take five in the morning and five at night, happily, they were twenty-five per cent less potent than the former ones but I also had anti sickness drugs and steroids to take. I had high hopes that I'd feel a lot better than I did before. I was disappointed, no sooner had I started taking the medication than I was sick. I really did try hard to find ways of keeping the medicine and food down. I'd start with porridge or tomato soup and then take the tablets. But often I'd retch and vomit it all up! Very late one evening I had to phone the out of hours' duty doctor because I was in such a bad way. He came to the house and gave me an injection to address the severe symptoms and asked me what kind of cancer I had. 'Oesophageal,' I replied. 'I'm so sorry to hear that,' he said, evidently understanding the serious nature of the disease.

Although people were praying for me, a small group of Christians decided to set up a regular time when they could pray and fast for God's intervention. Their first meeting was on 6 December. They worshipped and prayed together and God encouraged them through scriptures, songs and pictures.

While I was grateful for my friends' support, I also struggled with it. The fact was that when people prayed, my symptoms got worse. Occasionally the battle became so severe that I actually asked them to stop praying – they ignored me and carried on.

Up until now I'd been using Sue's Internet access, but in early December I ordered a new laptop. What I was really saying was, 'I'm still fighting for a future.' It arrived on 7 December and a few days later James, my nephew, kindly bought me a dongle to go with it. It felt good to be in the twenty-first century at last!

I had my third chemo infusion on 10 December. By then I was counting down the days to the last day of the month when the chemotherapy would end. My body couldn't cope with the pills which I had concluded would kill me well before the cancer! I felt drained, in pain and breathless and I wondered how I could possibly keep going.

Support from all quarters was helping to sustain me. I had almost daily visits from family members and Mary, from the Macmillan Community Team visited me weekly to give me a foot massage; she was always cheerful, positive and full of fun. My work colleagues gave me cards and gifts which made me cry because I felt so isolated and apart from them. I received a lot of support from my church friends who sent me cards and flowers and prayed for me. My counsellor, Irene, was visiting me every week and so too was Steve, one of the church elders.

At night time Mum and I adopted a new routine. We'd lie in bed and think of all the things that we could thank God for. We'd thank him for the warm safe home he'd given us; for the sunshine; for the nature programme that we'd watched on TV; for the robin we'd noticed in the garden and for the moon and the stars that we could see through the window. It was all very simple – we just wanted to be grateful. I recall one occasion when I warbled on for about ten minutes, wished Mum good night and heard a distinct snore emanating from her bed. But there were some nights when I couldn't pray. Then I sat in bed and quietly pleaded, 'Lord, let me die in the night.' I was disappointed when I'd come to in the early hours, still trapped in an endless waking nightmare.

At this, my lowest point, I used my new laptop to look on the Internet for ways of committing suicide. It was a bitterly cold winter and I concluded that the easiest way would be to wait until Mum was out and simply walk onto the South Downs. I'd already decided on the remote location. When I got there, I'd simply lie down in the snow and fall asleep. I was in a quandary about the idea. Could I really do this to my family? What would they understand by my actions? But it seemed the only way out of my suffering and my mind was made up. One day I wrote a note, packed a small bag of things that were precious to me and waited for an opportunity. My plans were thwarted when later, in the early evening; I began suffering from excruciating pain in my lungs and chest. I phoned the hospital and explained the situation. 'Can you get yourself here and see one of the duty doctors?' they asked me. Neither Mum nor I wanted to drive so we took a taxi. The doctors were naturally concerned not to interfere with any medication that I was already taking, so they couldn't do much for me. After this episode, there was no way in which I could have walked onto the Downs to end my life. So for the next couple of days I resorted to asking God to help me to cope with what was happening.

Mum desperately needed a break so I went to stay with Sue and her husband, Mike, for about three days. I was gagging on the chemo tablets, battling with the fear that food was getting stuck in the stent and trying to get through each day until the end of December when the chemotherapy medication would stop. I was also trying hard to tack some sort of normality into my life, so I went with Sue to buy their Christmas tree, and also for a ten minute walk in the snow. Christmas trees and walks were so familiar but I was feeling anything but normal. Festive decorations meant nothing to me, food didn't mean anything either. The prescribed fortified drinks which were supposed to give me the nutrients that I needed tasted horrible and made me retch, so I abandoned them. I was having to force myself to 'do this, do that'; I resembled a zombie.

At that time I was reading extracts from a newspaper by a notable author who'd been diagnosed with oesophageal cancer six months earlier. I really identified with him when he outlined some of his battles, both big and small. For example, a sudden ambush by a bank card through the post which leaves you questioning, 'which one of us will reach its expiry date first?' By late December I was coping marginally better with the stent but I was still very depressed and had no desire to celebrate Christmas – I couldn't face the fact that it might be my last. On 25 December Mum joined Sue and her family in Hassocks for two hours, and Jane left her family and spent some time with me. We just sat and talked until Mum returned.

Dr Robinson phoned on 29 December, two days before the end of the chemotherapy programme. 'How's it gone?' he asked me. Then he added, 'You needn't bother with the last two days of the chemo pills.' But I was determined to complete the course, just as an act of defiance against the cancer. After the final dose I took the packaging out into the back garden, set fire to it and leapt up and down on what was left. Mum watched and laughed with me.

CHAPTER 6

THE SHADOW OF DEATH

My body thoroughly enjoyed its New Year's treat: no more rotten chemo pills. Within a few days I was feeling heaps better and was tucking into soft foods and rejoicing that I wouldn't be revisited by them! As a way of celebration I even went for the occasional short drive in my car, something that I'd missed.

The doctors wanted to know what effect the chemotherapy had had on me so on 5 January I went to the hospital for a CT scan of my thorax and abdomen. I was convinced that my violent reaction to the tablets was proof that the chemotherapy was doing its work and shrinking the tumour. The next step would be a major operation at the end of the month. It was now my mission to build myself up and get as fit as I could for that. Naturally, I was keen to know when I would have the surgery. On 12 January the hospital multi-disciplinary team were meeting to discuss the CT results, so I rang Veronica later that day to see if there was a date for the operation. Her reply slightly perplexed me. 'I'm not allowed to tell you one way or another what was discussed at the meeting – you'll have to wait to see Dr Robinson in a couple of weeks.' I assumed that her reluctance to answer my question was because she knew that I'd need more chemotherapy and feared my reaction. So when Mum and I returned to the hospital on 20 January, I was expecting delay, not devastation. Veronica was in the room when my oncologist, Dr Robinson dropped the bombshell. 'The chemotherapy has had no effect at all on the tumour,' he said, 'and we're now seeing new growth in your lungs. The cancer is spreading round your body and we're unable to operate. It's terminal. I'm so sorry but we can't do any more for you. You need to go home and put your affairs in order.' 'How long have I got?' I asked. 'A matter of months,' he replied. 'At the outside you might just make it to Christmas.'

Mum and I went into a side room with Veronica who, like us, was very upset. She'd really been hoping that things would turn out well for me. We just sat with her, stunned. 'I'll have to make a will and sell my house' I said, thinking out loud. Veronica asked, 'Is there anywhere you'd like to go and visit while you still can?' 'No' came my reply; the prospect of taking a holiday and being away from my family wasn't anywhere in my thinking. Veronica stayed with us for about thirty minutes. Then Mum and I left – discharged from the hospital's care as those who could no longer be helped through medical means.

Back at home I immediately phoned my sisters. The following day I contacted close friends and colleagues and none of them could believe the diagnosis. Most thought that the chemotherapy and operation would solve the problem and give me at the very least a few more years to live. I was all too aware that I would not be around to enjoy another Christmas. For some years the kitchen calendar was where Mum often expressed her feelings about things that happened. A good day was marked with a tick and a bad day, a cross. Particularly good or bad days were given extra ticks or crosses – so you could have a four tick day or a two cross day. When we got back from the hospital Mum wrote six crosses against 20 January. Suddenly she was grappling with the prospect that she was going to see her youngest daughter die.

Things developed quickly after my terminal diagnosis. I made the decision that my house should go on the market and within two days my family were preparing it for the estate agent – just making it presentable for him to take photos and make a valuation. He came on 26 January and Mum and I were there to receive him. I didn't tell him why I was selling my house because I feared that a potential buyer might take advantage of my desire for a quick sale. Ignorant of my personal circumstances, and keen to gain new business, he wondered if his company could help me to purchase another property in the area. 'No that's all right, thank you,' said, Mum, 'she's moving up!' At that comment Mum and I exchanged a glance – half smile, half grimace. The poor man didn't quite know what to make of this quick-fire remark and didn't pursue it further.

It was emotionally hard for me to sell my house. Nineteen years previously Mum and Dad had helped me to buy it and, with the assistance of family and friends, much had been done over the years to make it look really nice. It was in a sunny position and I'd had some great neighbours and lots of happy memories. Over the years I'd had a number of lodgers and my spare room got the reputation of being the place to stay if you wanted to become a potential bride! It was a house full of fun and laughter – just like my early childhood. On one occasion I'd invited some work friends for a meal and had accidentally dropped the chicken as I was getting it out of the oven. We watched, slack-jawed as it sailed across the vinyl and then laughed till we had tears streaming down our faces – and we still ate it! All the house needed was a new carpet here and there. Instead, I was being forced to sell it and after a few days it was on the open market.

Financially, I was in a good position. I'd been paid a full salary for a few months and then Statutory Sick Pay until the end of December 2010. I then began receiving a couple of benefits, including Disability Living Allowance. My employer continued to regard me as a staff member, indeed, my job at the YMCA was held open irrespective of what was happening and I was told that if I died in service my dependents would receive a sum several times my annual salary. My colleagues were nothing but supportive and immediately after my terminal diagnosis I received another raft of cards from them. The Board of Management and some of my colleagues were praying. David, my boss and Vanessa visited me now and again to update me on what was happening at work and to pray and encourage me.

I was very close to my nine nieces and nephews. Sarah, one of my nieces, was getting married in April and although living in London, she'd chosen a dress in a shop in Brighton. She'd agreed to meet Mum, Sue and me at the shop on 5 February for a fitting – seeing as I might not be able to attend her wedding day. The experience was almost unbearable; I sat there looking on, and silently wept. Flooding into my mind were memories of the fun that Sarah and I had shared together (she'd lived with me for a year whilst studying at university) and now the prospect of not being able to see her marry and watch her future unfold was too much to take.

It was challenging to make a will. There was such a sense of finality about it. I told the solicitor that I wasn't well enough to attend his office, so he came to Mum's house on 7 February. I explained to him exactly what was happening and he was kind to me, saying that he really didn't know what to say. He drafted the will and finalised it on a second visit. I used his firm in the sale of my house.

I was fast hitting rock bottom. Physically I was in a lot of pain down through my core and in my back, which only a combination of liquid morphine and slow release morphine tablets kept at bay. I was also becoming more and more breathless. Emotionally I was drowning, struggling with the loss of everything: my health, my ability to eat, a job that I loved, my home, independent living and my family (especially Mum who at seventy-four was increasingly vulnerable) and friends – not to mention my very life. Everything was being stripped away; I felt that God had abandoned me.

Even in the shadow of death, I continued to receive incredible support from my family and friends. I recognised the courage of those who came to visit me – it couldn't have been easy for them to engage with someone who was within months of dying. These times together were precious, although bitter sweet. On one occasion Steve and his wife, Rosey prayed for me and I sensed the presence and love of God for the first time in ages. Some people persisted in praying for my healing. Others, on the assumption that God was taking me to be with him in heaven, prayed more along the lines of a good death than for his miraculous intervention. I was grateful for and welcomed all their prayers, whatever the motivation behind them.

By this time, only family members and very close friends were visiting me. They didn't realise it, but on paper I'd distributed my possessions among them. And when they came to see me I told them how much I loved them. I think that they guessed what was really happening: I was saying 'Goodbye.'

CHAPTER 7

THE MARTLETS

Before Christmas 2010 one of the MacMillan nurses had suggested that I might like to visit the Day Centre at the Martlets Hospice in Hove. I turned down her invitation, at that time I was having chemotherapy and battling with extreme sickness and I simply didn't think that I could cope with anything else. Besides, back in December, I believed that I was in with a fighting chance of getting better. Now that I'd been given my terminal diagnosis, I was willing to receive palliative care, which is continuing support when cure is no longer possible. It involves symptom control and living to the full until the moment you die.

My first encounter with the Martlets was on 8 February 2011. Mum drove me there and stayed with me all day. Walking into the building was quietly devastating; an acknowledgment that my life was coming to an end. I looked around and thought, 'I'm one of the patients here.' It was so unreal. I expected the place to be sombre but I was pleasantly surprised. We were met by some very friendly staff members and were offered tea, coffee, biscuits and cake. Julie, my dedicated nurse, showed me around. Although I'd be visiting weekly, I saw the bedrooms of the in-patients which were light and airy, with views either onto an inner courtyard or onto an attractive garden on the perimeter. I couldn't help but wonder, 'Which of these rooms will I die in?' I'd already decided that I didn't want to die at home. At the end of the corridor there was a family bedroom where your loved ones could stay to be with you. That idea was both comforting and grim at one and the same time.

The Day Centre was open plan with a sitting and dining area with views onto the courtyard, a small kitchen in one corner and an art and craft section in the other. There was a separate conservatory at the back. Lunch was served at a long table and the chef prepared food to suit each patient. You could even have a glass of wine with your meal if you wanted. Contrary to my expectations, I felt at ease there. The building had a relaxed, calm atmosphere and the staff were knowledgeable and empathetic. I noticed copies of *The Daily Telegraph* and the local *Argus* on a table in the lounge and felt comforted, these were the papers that Mum and I read at home. In the weeks to come, I regularly vied with another patient as to which of us could get to *The Telegraph* first! The staff, volunteers and patients were all really welcoming and by the time Mum and I left I was thinking, 'This is a safe space. I can cope with this. It will give Mum a break too.'

I'd only driven a couple of times since the New Year, so every Tuesday I was reliant on the Martlets' minibus for transportation. I had to be ready by 9:00am, although the minibus didn't necessarily arrive at that time, it depended on where I was on the pick-up list. Sometimes there'd be only four or five individuals on the minibus, sometimes seven or eight. On board there was a cheery driver and a volunteer who went from person to person taking down lunch orders; there was a pretty exhaustive menu choice. The minibus could be a very emotional place. Sometimes it was the centre of a great deal of fun and banter, while on others its occupants might be feeling very low, suffering pain and/or feeling sick. They could also be heart-wrenching, as I discovered in the early days. One woman we picked up lived on the road parallel to mine and I found it hard to ride along familiar streets knowing that the house I loved was on the market. Then we'd drive near Hove Park School where I was once a pupil. I'd watch the children walking home and feel totally shut out from any kind of normal existence. It just seemed to accentuate the fact that I was on the outside looking in.

Tuesday was actually the day for the younger people, although at that point in time our ages ranged from about forty up to around sixty-five. As I continued to attend I became captivated by the loving atmosphere and looked forward to my weekly visits. We'd all been thrown together for one reason and accepted each other unconditionally. I thoroughly enjoyed the new relationships that I made both with staff members and patients. The Martlets was a place where you could be yourself.

I quickly slotted into the 10:00am to 3:00pm Tuesday routine (extended by the minibus trips). Sometimes there were about ten patients at the Martlets, sometimes fewer. The recliner chairs in the lounge were sheer luxury and it seemed that wherever you were you'd be plied with tea, coffee or biscuits. If you wanted to have a quiet day, others would leave you alone to read. But if you wanted company, there was plenty of that too. The patients were encouraged to make the best of the day and there were some regular activities that we could engage in: hand, leg and foot massages, painting, and relaxation therapy. An older volunteer came in several times to paint nails. On one occasion a singing group entertained us. On another, a young woman played her violin. If you didn't want to be involved in any of these you could simply sit quietly, shut your eyes and have a rest, read or go outside to the courtyard for a walk and maybe a cigarette. I decided early on to learn to paint with watercolours, ably taught by Gordon, an auxiliary nurse. At lunchtimes most of us sat together round a table like a family and the volunteers waited on us. There was a starter, a main course and a dessert, but if all you wanted was a piece of toast, that was available too. The food was excellent and there was no pressure on what or how much you ate. Some might have hearty appetites while others were nibbling like birds. We all understood: the actual process of dying is hard.

Every two weeks the patients would see an in-house Consultant or a Lead Clinical Nurse. These staff members were very supportive, having embraced the hospice's values, namely a holistic approach to life. They checked both our medication and also our emotional and spiritual needs and enquired whether everything was OK at home. I realised that they could meet any medical needs very fast, which naturally gave me a stronger sense of security there than when I was at home. Each Tuesday seemed to consist of a strange blend of comedy and tragedy and I got used to seeing a mix of emotions in the same room. One minute one of my new friends who was on steroids was joking about having demolished a whole packet of sausage rolls the night before and was on the lookout for more! The next minute I was watching the distraught husband of two young children as he sat beside his wife, only a year older than me, who was slowly dying of the same cancer that had killed another family relative.

It wasn't hard to get to know other patients because stark reality made us more prone to sharing our thoughts and feelings. It was easy to tell them and the staff, 'I'm a Christian'; it was equally easy to add, 'but I'm scared of what the process of dying is going to be like.' I couldn't always be so candid with my family or my Christian friends.

We lived with the inevitability of death and after discussion with medical staff, I signed a DNR (Do Not Resuscitate) document. Sometimes several weeks would go by without any of my friends dying. Then several would seem to die at once. People who became very sick would often go to the Martlets' Inpatient Unit or, if there were no beds available, they'd be transferred to the Oncology Ward at the Royal Sussex Hospital. They'd sometimes go downhill very quickly after that. No-one needed to make an announcement if one of the group had died. A staff member would light a candle and put it in the lounge along with a card bearing the person's name. I must have lost six or seven friends while I was there. Tuesday became the highlight of the week. In spite of the suffering around me at the Martlets I enjoyed the companionship and was sad when I had to return home. Mum benefitted from the free day too. It gave her a breathing space during a week which was otherwise relentlessly hard for both of us.

At home I was battling on all fronts: physically, mentally and emotionally. I was on slow release morphine for the pain and anti-depressants. I wasn't eating much and felt breathless when I tried to go upstairs. I walked like an old woman, rarely dressed in outdoor clothes, spent most of my time in bed and looked absolutely dreadful. The cancer was taking over, but I resolved to die well.

CHAPTER 8

WORDS OF HOPE

I never knew how to thank my friends and family enough for their support through every stage of my battle. Not only did they visit, pray and fast for me, many of them also brought me words of encouragement from God. I relished those encouragements more than anything else.

What few people knew was that God had already spoken to me back in June 2010 immediately after I was first signed off sick from the YMCA and before I knew that I had cancer. At the time I was arguing my case with him. I desperately wanted a permanent breakthrough from the unending cycle of inner turmoil – over three decades of it. In the quietness of my bedroom he told me that he'd soon bring a watershed in my life, ordering a time for my enduring release. Like Jacob, I was wrestling, but in my case it was initially against deep depression and anxiety. In the light of this, a prophecy from the book of Isaiah in the Bible also raised my hopes:

'Why do you say, O Jacob ... "My way is hidden from the LORD; my cause is disregarded by my God"? Do you not know? Have you not heard? The LORD is the everlasting God, the Creator of the ends of the earth ... He gives strength to the weary and increases the power of the weak...' (Isaiah 40:27-29).

These verses were a real encouragement to me, but the ones which meant even more appeared in the next chapter of Isaiah:

'So do not fear, for I am with you; do not be dismayed, for I am your God. I will strengthen you and help you; I will uphold you

with my righteous right hand. All who rage against you will surely be ashamed and disgraced; those who oppose you will be as nothing and perish. Though you search for your enemies, you will not find them. Those who wage war against you will be as nothing at all...' (Is. 41:10-12).

Later I personalised the message: 'The cancer that opposes you will be as nothing and perish. Though you search for it, you will not find it. The cancer that wages war against you will be as nothing at all.'

It was Dodie Osteen's book, *Healed of Cancer* (Harrison House, 1987) that gave me further hope. A friend had leant it to me in January 2011 and immediately I started reading it I was struck by Dodie's faith. It was a really short but accessible book and I identified with her struggles with terminal liver cancer and her reliance on the Word of God. I had nothing else to hold onto and this book stirred me to read the Bible more and allow it to impact my life. I read from it constantly.

Dodie highlighted the importance of standing on God's promises and I began to meditate on many of the scriptures that she suggested and took greater care in what I declared with my mouth. God was renewing my mind and the result was a greater sense of peace, a greater awe of God and a greater desire to be thankful to him regardless of what happened.

By now five church members (who could be nicknamed the Famous Five), plus my sister Sue, had committed to meet weekly on Monday evenings at Mum's house to pray for me. We would spend time praising and worshipping God and listening to what he was saying. No evening was ever the same. Sue arrived one day with a packet of mustard seeds and gave one to each person present saying, 'That's as much faith as God requires of us'. The irony of this was that *Mustard Seed* was the name of the church youth group that I belonged to in my late teens. Sue had also learnt from a physiotherapist colleague that God was healing people of cancer in California, so I went online and watched several video testimonies.

One of those testimonies concerned a man in his fifties who was in the early stages of oesophageal cancer. He'd gone to *Bethel Church Healing Rooms*, California and a young boy had prayed for his healing. He was offended that he'd travelled for many hours only to be prayed for by a mere child. As others joined in, he had an amazing feeling of love and power running though his body. When he went for a scan he was told that there was a bright light shining from his oesophagus which was interfering with the image. A second scan revealed that one of the tumours had shrunk and the other was now benign. Later his doctors confirmed that he was cancer-free.

Naturally, listening to this man's testimony caused my faith to rise. I wanted to be where God was working so on 4 February the family booked an online Skype prayer slot at the *Healing Rooms*. We must have been a sight for sore eyes: a small family group at Sue's house, huddled around her little laptop, waiting expectantly for the call to come. When we got connected a young man, complete with dreadlocks, spent a couple of minutes praying for me. There was no change in my condition, but my contact with Bethel led me along a new pathway, thanks to my sister Jane. On hearing what was happening in California, she recalled an event from a couple of years previously. Jane's husband had been at a small church in Petworth, West Sussex and had heard a visiting pastor from New Zealand called Craig Marsh who'd been miraculously healed of stomach cancer in 1999. From that time he felt commissioned by God to pray for others to be healed and had travelled extensively to that end. I found his story on YouTube and totally identified with him as he related his experiences, which were packed with humour. I laughed out loud – the first time I'd done that for ages. Immediately I recalled a sermon that I'd heard several years before. The preacher had challenged the congregation by asking, 'What makes you so special that God can't intervene on your behalf?' I'd never heard that argument before. He was suggesting that it was actually arrogant to set yourself apart as uniquely out of God's orbit. That evening God planted a seed of faith in my heart. For the first time I began thinking, 'If God can heal Craig, why can't he heal me?' It was a turning point in my life.

That same day, 9 February, I e-mailed Craig asking him to pray for me. Much to my surprise he replied by return. He told me that he and his wife were ministering in Sydney, Australia and that they and the church there would certainly pray for me. What I didn't know at the time was how miraculous that reply really was. Later he told me that he often received up to ninety e-mails a day and had no time to read them all. But on 9 February he opened his laptop between ministry sessions and glanced over dozens of e-mails. The one that caught his attention had the subject line: 'Prayer Request for Healing of Oesophageal Cancer' and it was from me.

Meanwhile, I continued to wrestle over the stent. What if something really was stuck in it? I was so much in need of reassurance that I plagued the Digestive Diseases staff into giving me a second barium swallow just to check that everything was OK. Dr Davis obliged. 'There's nothing stuck,' he assured me. He'd obviously looked at my hospital notes and had seen my prognosis because he then added, 'It's bad, isn't it?'

The days passed and I heard no further word from Craig, so on 25 February I wrote to him again asking him when he would next be coming to the UK. My e-mail was met with more silence. I e-mailed Craig again on 2 March and he replied with the devastating news, 'sadly at this stage we may not be making it to the UK... for the first time in 11 years.' It was clear that he had no finances to come to England and he seemed reticent to travel so far for just one person. In addition, he was due to have a hernia operation at about this time and a visit to see me in 2011 was really out of the question. Immediately I began wondering if I could fly out to New Zealand to see him with Sue as my chaperone – but it was always a crazy idea. I was simply too weak to travel anywhere and no insurance company would ever have agreed to cover me on such a trip.

On 3 March I e-mailed Craig again: 'To be honest I'm finding it difficult to get to walk around the block or down to the shops. Just getting out of bed is a struggle and I'm also suffering from severe depression/anxiety. I've had bouts of this over the years since my 20s and they've always been around the fear of not being able to eat, or sustain myself and choking to death. I'm really struggling and wrestling with

God at the prospect of an early death and the manner of it – the last 6 months have been very traumatic and frightening. I'm not worried about where I'm going but I really fear the physicality of death... Basically what I'm trying to say, but not very well, is that coming out to NZ would be the act of a desperate woman but one who still believes in a big and merciful God who is able to heal anything.'

The 8 March fell on a Tuesday, it was my forty-fourth birthday. I'd told my family and friends that I didn't wish to mark the day and specifically requested no cards or presents. I didn't want anyone at the Martlets to know about it either. Nevertheless, after lunch the staff produced a card and some cupcakes and celebrated it anyway. Deep down I was glad that they'd remembered.

At about this time I made a conscious decision not to look any more at the reams of information on oesophageal cancer on the Internet. But I wondered what death meant for an oesophageal cancer patient, so I asked the Martlets' consultant, 'What can I expect? What will the physical process of dying involve?' She'd told me, 'In the last stages you'll probably stop eating, your pain will increase but will be controlled, you'll get more tired and sleepy and will then fall into unconsciousness.' On reflection, I actually found this idea quite comforting because I was likely to be in a coma when I slipped into eternity.

On 10 March I received a prayer cloth from Craig. Earlier he'd told me, 'We've seen many miracles happen as a result (of people wearing it)'. I wore it 24/7, which was a bit of a problem at the Martlets. I understand that when patients with a serious illness receive bad news, they can use denial as a coping mechanism. So when the hospice Consultant was giving me a physical examination, she saw the prayer cloth pinned to my inner clothing and immediately assumed that I'd blocked out her earlier comments and wasn't accepting the unavoidable consequences of my disease. I could understand her concerns. Healing from terminal cancer was unheard of at the Martlets. In her eyes I needed to be peacefully resigned to my inevitable fate. But I was still determined to wear the prayer cloth! I told Sue what the Consultant had said and she was determined to prove her wrong. Sue's motivation was spurred on by the testimonies that we'd been hearing from California. People were being healed of terminal cancer and God was great enough to heal me too. Fuelled by a strong sense of indignation she phoned some friends who'd attended a church in Lindfield which had links with Craig. They suggested that she spoke to the pastor who offered to phone Craig on her behalf.

I knew that I was in a win-win situation. The Bible told me that after death I could expect everlasting life and I believed it. If I died I knew that I'd be with Jesus and enjoy the ultimate healing. But Dodie's book was challenging me. 'She survived against the odds.' I thought. 'God can heal me too. I don't want to die aged forty-four and leave my family and friends behind.' And with that, I and others continued to argue the case with God.

CHAPTER 9

GOOD NEWS

God continued to orchestrate support for me from all directions. When I was struggling with the chemotherapy my friends Tracy and Aafje had sprung into action and soon a whole raft of e-mails was being cascaded into the inboxes of those church members who knew me well. These e-mails contained updates on my progress and specific prayer requests. At about this time God had brought two other key people into the mix, Jan and Christine. Jan was from a local Methodist Church, had served as a hospital chaplain, and had such a radiant face that mum likened her to an angel arriving at the front door! Christine, a member of my church, had set up the Martlets Day Hospice years earlier and was now retired. Their primary concern was to give Mum support and their friendship and wisdom proved invaluable.

Christine firmly believed that hospice care embraced the whole family, so she put this into practice through pastoral visits. When she first came to our house I was in my dressing gown leaning heavily against the kitchen door for support. She told me later, 'Your face was wincing with discomfort and you were hardly able to concentrate on greeting me. I knew from my nursing background that you were extremely sick and your symptoms revealed that you were in the end stages of life.'

Every Thursday morning Christine and Mum would go into the summer house for a coffee and a chat. Their conversations covered a wide range of topics, but frequently slipped into the subject of my illness and how hard it was to keep going when your daughter was so unwell. Mum had always been a regular churchgoer, believed in God and Jesus and would have said that she was a Christian. But to her, God was remote and strict. This really concerned me. I was facing death and wanted to be sure that I'd see her again in heaven. Had she really made a personal commitment to him? Christine chatted to her about this and later that day I followed up on their conversation.

It was a bright, sunny day. We were lying on Mum's bed and I was in my night clothes, which was now normal for me. I picked up the booklet, *Journey into Life*, and went through it with her. She prayed the prayer of commitment on the back page and I was elated. About twenty minutes later I felt so ill (because my medication was being modified) that I put my head over the hand basin in her bedroom and was violently sick!

It was so good to have the faithful support of my family and friends. One evening I arrived (like an old cripple) at one of the prayer meetings and was moved to see about eighteen friends from my church who'd gathered to pray for me. But another meeting that I'll never forget was on 28 March, when the usual Monday night women's prayer group met together at Tracy's house. Actually, I almost didn't attend. I was in such pain that the staff at the Martlets were thinking of accommodating me for a couple of nights while they readjusted my medication. I felt as though I could die within the following few weeks. But I decided to go anyway. Sue drove me to the house. We always started our prayer times worshipping God, then waited to see what he'd do. On this particular evening, Irene prayed particularly passionately and Valerie read and commented on a scripture from the book of Joshua:

'Now Jericho was shut up inside and outside because of the people of Israel. None went out, and none came in. And the Lord said to Joshua, "See, I have given Jericho into your hand, with its king and mighty men of valour"' (Joshua 6:1, 2).

Essentially, God was speaking in terms of the impossible. Jericho was a veritable fortress, but he'd delivered it into the hands of the Israelites. As far as he was concerned, it was a done deal, declared in the past tense, even though the victory hadn't physically been won. What the Israelites had to do was obey what he told them, even if his instructions (walking round the city seven times) made absolutely no sense at all. Valerie stressed that winning this battle would not necessarily follow the normal pattern. No matter what we saw in front of us we'd need to listen to God, pray as he directed and do whatever he said. Only then would we gain the victory.

Julie announced that God had given her a picture of a highway made of little yellow bricks. 'From now on he just wants you to put one foot in front of the other,' she said. 'It's not a sprint. It's a steady walk.' The word, 'highway' also dovetailed into this picture really well. Isaiah tells us that on God's highway *'No lion will be there, nor will any ferocious beast get up on it; they will not be found there... the redeemed... will enter Zion with singing; everlasting joy will crown their heads. Gladness and joy will overtake them, and sorrow and sighing will flee away'* (Is 35:8-10). There was wide open road ahead of me.

When the group started praying for me someone asked, 'Is God saying anything to you, Liz?' Now I was in a dilemma. God suddenly brought a particular secret sin to my mind but I didn't want anyone to know about it. I wrestled with my answer and finally decided, 'If God is here how can I be so proud as to block his blessing?' With that, I confessed my sin to him and the group and repented. What happened next was extraordinary, almost on a par with Acts 2 when the New Testament believers were first filled with the Holy Spirit. A power came over me and I found myself almost unable to contain an incredible energy. I just couldn't stand still. If it hadn't been cold and dark outside, I'd have zoomed out into the garden. Instead, I raced around Steve and Tracy's dining room table about thirty times, much to the astonishment of the assembled company. The irony wasn't lost on them: I'd walked into the house bent over like an old woman having sent them e-mails to say that I was at death's door. And now look at me!

From that evening the blackness that had shrouded me like a thick impenetrable cloak started to lift and the chronic clinical depression simply evaporated. Yes, in the eyes of others I still seemed to get depressed, but in reality it was an appropriate sadness given my cancer diagnosis. Strangely, the energy that I experienced that evening was with me only momentarily; I was still physically extremely unwell.

Sarah, my niece was due to be married on 9 April and I was appealing to God, 'Please don't take me before her wedding.' In the early hours of that morning I awoke with a prolonged and severe coughing fit which left me gasping for air. I'd slid down my bed and inhaled some of my stomach contents into my lungs and now I was struggling to catch my breath. Mum phoned the paramedics but by the time they arrived I'd recovered. By now I was displaying some of the symptoms of advanced disease: severe pain, fatigue, loss of appetite, a pallor and puffiness in my face, and pins and needles in my hands due to fluid retention.

The wedding was held in Camden, London. Mum travelled up with Jane and Alan, her husband, leaving me lying in bed and attended by Rosey, the wife of Steve who was one of my church elders. After about twenty minutes she looked at me and said, 'Come on, Liz. Let's go for it. Get dressed and see how you feel.' I was still breathing so I thought, 'Why not?' Rosey sent a text to Steve asking him to muster some prayer support! So we got into her car and started out for London.

When we were about twenty minutes away from the venue I phoned Mum saying that we were on our way. Jane was waiting on the kerbside for us. We arrived after the marriage ceremony but before the photos in the square opposite. Rosey had planned to wander around Camden until I was ready to return, but we were all very keen for her to stay and happily included her at the reception. The family was delighted that I was there, but was equally struggling with the unmentionable prospect that we'd never be together like this again. Rosey drove Mum and me home. As we sped down the motorway I had an incredible sense of future. I simply couldn't see myself being dead in the next few weeks or months with the traditional candle and card in the Martlets lounge for my friends to remember me.

The day after the wedding James, my nephew, called round. 'This is for you, Liz,' he said. I'd just spent the whole day lying on my bed and suddenly deposited in my hand was a shiny medal imprinted with the words Brighton Marathon, 10 April 2011. James had run the race for me; he was exhausted and in a lot of pain; his feet were badly blistered but he wanted me to have the prize. I was stunned and deeply touched.

It had been a wonderful family weekend, but the thought that Craig wouldn't be visiting the UK was a blow. Then, a few days later, Sue bounced excitedly through the front door, found me, grabbed me by the shoulders and declared, 'I've got news for you. Craig Marsh is coming!'

GASTROSCOPY REPORT

Name: **Elizabeth Woodgate, 08/03/1967 (F)** Address:
NHS No:
Case note no.:

Procedure date
13th September 2010

GP: A Mahony
Hove Medical Centre

Priority: Urgent
Status: Outpatient/NHS
Hospital: RSCH

Referring Cons:
(Medicine)

Indications
Abnormality on barium.

Consultant/Endoscopist
Consultant:
Endoscopist No1:
Endoscopist No2:
Nurses:

Report
The procedure was completed successfully.
Apparent mucosal junction at 40cm from the incisors.
OESOPHAGUS. Exophytic tumour, adenocarcinoma, resulting in stricture
with luminal narrowing and at (a).
STOMACH. Polyps: benign submucosal 4mm at (b).

OTHER

Instrument
Loan endoscope

Diagnoses
OESOPHAGUS. Malignant tumour and stricture.
STOMACH. Polyp.
DUODENUM. Normal.

Premedication
Midazolam (IV) 3 mg

Follow up
Awaiting pathology results. Notes to
UGI MDM coordinator.

Advice/comments
Exophytic circumferential friable tumour at 35cm ab oral.
It appeared to extend beyond the GOJ clearly visible on
retroflexion.There was considerable luminal narrowing of
the distal oesophagus. There was a small submucosal
lesion in the antrum with central ulcer- ? GIST. Normal
duodenum. CT CAP requested . Will need EUS/PET. I
have suggested soft diet.

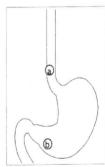

a: *Lower oesophagus*
b: *Antrum*

Consultant Gastroenterologist

Specimens taken
Biopsy (x8 site a)

*Report showing the place and extent of Liz's tumour after her initial
scan*

THE SUSSEX CANCER CENTRE

Dr D Bloomfield	Dr G Newman
Dr A Nikapota	Dr A Ring
Dr D Gilbert	Dr A Robinson
Dr A Hiersche	Dr R Simcock
Dr R Langley	Dr J Simpson
Dr K Lankester	Dr A Webb
Dr F McKinna	Dr S Westwell
Dr S Mitra	Dr M Wilkins

Royal Sussex County Hospital
Eastern Road
Brighton
East Sussex
BN2 5BE

Tel: 01273 696955

☎ 01273 696955 Fax: 01273 623312

Trust Patient ID:
NHS No:

Ref: AR/sk/WS ID:
Date: 14 Oct 2010

Miss Elizabeth Woodgate

Dear Miss Woodgate

It was a pleasure to meet you in my clinic on the 14th October. Balancing all the various considerations regarding your cancer and the most appropriate treatment, I think we should try to commence some chemotherapy as soon as possible with the drugs Oxaliplatin and Capecitabine. I think   gave you an information sheet on a 3-drug combination of Epirubicin, Oxaliplatin and Capecitabine, but I'm not certain that the Epirubicin will add anything extra and does unfortunately come with a cost of hair loss.

I have booked you a follow up appointment in my clinic for around 4 weeks time to monitor how you are getting on with the chemotherapy and we can make any adjustments once we have started if you start to experience any toxicities. With kind regards.

Yours sincerely

Not signed to avoid delay

Dr A Robinson
Consultant in Clinical Oncology

cc   Dr A Mahoney
Hove Medical Centre

Letter from Consultant Oncologist to Liz prescribing her first course of chemotherapy'

X-ray showing Liz's oesophageal stent in place

Brighton and Sussex **NHS**
University Hospitals
NHS Trust

The Sussex Cancer Centre

Dr David Bloomfield   Dr Ashok Nikapota
Dr Anthony Chalmers   Dr Alistair Ring
Dr Andreas Hiersche   Dr Angus Robinson
Dr Ruth Langley   Dr Richard Simcock
Dr Kate Lankester   Dr Joanna Simpson
Dr Fiona McKinna   Dr Andrew Webb
Dr Sankha Mitra   Dr Sarah Westwell
Dr Geoffrey Newman   Dr Marie Wilkins

Secretary: frances.woodward@bsuh.nhs.uk
☎ 01273 664690 Fax: 01273 623312

Royal Sussex County Hospital
Eastern Road
Brighton
East Sussex
BN2 5BE

Tel: 01273 696955

Trust Patient ID:
NHS No:

Ref: AR/fw/WS ID:
Date: 11 Nov 2010

Dr. A Mahony
Hove Medical Centre

Dear Dr. Mahony

Re: Elizabeth Woodgate, DOB: 8/3/1967

Diagnosis: Bulky lower third carcinoma of the oesophagus
Oesophageal stent placement 28 October
Has commenced chemotherapy with Oxaliplatin and Capecitabine
on 29 October – marked toxicity
For dose adjustment and continued treatment

This lady returned to my oncology follow up clinic for review today. I was sorry to hear that she really has had a very tough time after the first dose of chemotherapy with marked nausea, sickness, fatigue, parasthesia and neurological Oxaliplatin related symptoms and diarrhoea. Her swallowing is good following the stent placement, but certainly she has felt increasingly unwell. I have advised no further chemotherapy for this cycle (she only managed 4 days of Capecitabine) and we will make some significant dose adjustments prior to cycle 2. I have arranged to see her again in early December following this second course of treatment to assess whether it will be possible for her to have any more treatment or whether in fact this really does not suit her at all.

cont'd......

Letter from Consultant Oncologist to GP after the failure of the first round of chemotherapy

Brighton and Sussex NHS
University Hospitals

NHS Trust

The Sussex Cancer Centre

Dr David Bloomfield	Dr Ashok Nikapota
Dr Anthony Chalmers	Dr Alistair Ring
Dr Andreas Hiersche	Dr Angus Robinson
Dr Ruth Langley	Dr Richard Simcock
Dr Kate Lankester	Dr Joanna Simpson
Dr Fiona McKinna	Dr Andrew Webb
Dr Sankha Mitra	Dr Sarah Westwell
Dr Geoffrey Newman	Dr Marie Wilkins

Secretary: frances.woodward@bsuh.nhs.uk
☎ 01273 664690 Fax: 01273 623312

Royal Sussex County Hospital
Eastern Road
Brighton
East Sussex
BN2 5BE

Tel: 01273 696955

Trust Patient ID:
NHS No:

Ref: AR/fw/WS ID:
Date: 29 Dec 2010
Typed: 5 Jan 2011

Dr. A Mahony
Hove Medical Centre

Dear Dr. Mahony

Re: Elizabeth Woodgate, DOB: 8/3/1967

Diagnosis: **Locally advanced lower third carcinoma of the oesophagus
Chemotherapy with Oxalyplatin and Capecitabine commenced end
of October 2010
3 cycles now completed
For repeat CT and further surgical discussion**

I had a telephone follow up consultation with this lady today. She was due to finish her chemotherapy in two days time, but in fact she is struggling with the Capecitabine medication and I have suggested that the final 48 hours are not necessary and she can stop this straight away.

The temporary stent she had positioned certainly helped with her swallowing and she is managing almost a normal diet, but she has run into quite significant problems with anxiety and depression once again.

We were very guarded about the operability of her primary tumour when she was diagnosed, but she will have a follow up CT scan to assess any evidence of response and her case will be discussed again at the multidisciplinary meeting with the upper GI surgeons present.

Letter from Consultant Oncologist to GP after third round of chemotherapy

Sussex Cancer Centre
Ref: DAR/FW/189905
Dictated: 27-Mar-2013
Typed: 27-Mar-2013

Royal Sussex County Hospital
Eastern Road
Brighton
East Sussex
BN2 5BE

Miss Elizabeth Woodgate

Tel: 01273 696955

Trust Patient ID:
NHS No:

Dear Miss Woodgate

It was a pleasure to catch up with you on the phone today. I just wanted to confirm in writing the plan.

As we discussed, the recent repeat CT scan shows no evidence of disease either in the oesophagus or in the lung. Clearly this is excellent news, but has raised questions about what the lung lesions that were previously seen were. We would therefore recommend some further tests with a repeat endoscopy and a PET CT scan to establish the state of the cancer currently in the oesophagus and indeed whether there is any disease further afield.

In addition the plain X-ray of the abdomen is also to look for where the stent has possibly migrated to.

I look forward to discussing and meeting again with the results of these extra tests in due course.

With kind regards

Yours sincerely

dictated but not checked or signed to avoid delay

Dr Angus Robinson
Consultant in Clinical Oncology

Letter from Consultant Oncologist confirming Liz is clear of cancer in the oesophagus and lungs

Sussex Cancer Centre
Ref: DAR/FW/336002
Dictated: 18-Jul-2013
Typed: 22-Jul-2013

Royal Sussex County Hospital
Eastern Road
Brighton
East Sussex
BN2 5BE

Dr A Mahony
Hove Medical Centre

Tel: 01273 696955

Trust Patient ID:
NHS No:

Dear Dr Mahony

Re: Elizabeth Woodgate, DOB: 08/03/1967

I caught up with Ms Woodgate and her friend in my oncology clinic today.

Just to recap her extraordinary story, she had a T3 N1 squamous cell cancer of the oesophagus diagnosed in 2010 and had three cycles of chemotherapy which were stopped because of the suspicion of lung secondaries. She had no further active oncological treatment, but 3 years later appears to be in remission (the lung lesions subsequently disappeared on further imaging).

She has done extraordinarily well and all her recent re-investigations show no evidence of recurrent or residual disease. Clearly this is a very unusual circumstance for oesophageal cancer, but we very much hope that this will be a durable response with no evidence of recurrence.

Certainly she is very fit and well and is keen to return to work.

I will see her intermittently in my follow-up clinic, but have not arranged any further investigations unless symptoms dictate. I have given her our contact details of the clinical nurse specialist based here at the hospital.

With kind regards

cont'd ......

Letter from Consultant Oncologist to GP 2½ years after treatment was ended

The Celebration cake with message, 'To God be the Glory, great things He has done'

CHAPTER 10

MOVING UP

I was trying hard to manage the delicate balance between the possibility of healing and the medical prognosis of death. 'She's moving up,' Mum had said to a puzzled estate agent, but I was now wondering whether 'up' meant heaven or more years on earth. I knew that God could intervene if he chose to do that. But the reality was that time was running out for me and death was only weeks away.

In addition, I was attempting to sort out my affairs because I didn't want my family to be burdened by them. I spent a lot of time on the phone to the bank, to insurance companies and to the local Council. I needed to cancel my mortgage payments, stop various standing orders and close all my savings accounts and put my money in one place to make everything easy. Time and time again I had to fend off the same enquiries from various professional bodies: 'Can we offer you support in the future?' 'What about one of our new mortgages on your next home?' We're confident that we can offer you a better deal.' When I told them that I might soon be dead, I was met with the same awkward silence and the comment, 'I'm so sorry, I don't know what to say.'

My house sold quickly and on 14 April the family helped me to clear the contents. One day Mum drove me to the estate agents so that I could sign various documents. When I returned to the car I had a pang of conscience. I'd kept the reason for the sale a secret but I just felt that I should come clean. 'I've got to go back, Mum,' I said. 'I must tell them why

I'm selling the house. I don't want to deceive them.' With that I returned to the office and explained that I had terminal cancer and had only a few months to live. Again, no one knew quite how to respond to me.

It wasn't easy to live between life and death. I was in a lot of pain. My face and hands were grey and puffy – evidence of the final stages of life, and the growing tumour made my breath smell foul. I had waves of nausea; there was a continual gurgle deep in my gullet and I was eating very little. I had no energy, the night sweats kept me awake and I spent most days either in bed or on the sofa. There seemed to be little point in getting dressed so I wore my nightwear nearly all the time. Basic activities like showering or washing my hair left me breathless; reading lost its appeal; I avoided talking to people and watched the TV with little enthusiasm. I was on ever-increasing doses of morphine and a whole stack of other pills and I felt awful. At night Mum would periodically check to see whether I was still alive. I wasn't. This wasn't life; it was a mere cocooned existence. My Tuesday visits to the Martlets were my only 'normal' activities – if you consider visits to a hospice to be in any way 'normal.'

What kept me from falling apart emotionally was my faith in God and the news that in three weeks Craig would be in the UK. It was a wonderful thought as I went to bed at night. I could hardly believe that God was sending him halfway round the world just for me – and immediately after he'd had recent surgery too. So why had he suddenly changed his mind about coming to the UK? Apparently, after his pastor friend in Lindfield had contacted him, he'd woken up one night and God had spoken to him, telling him that he should go to England to pray for me. He then phoned Sue and discussed when he could come. She remarked that it needed to be soon because my condition was deteriorating rapidly. He booked a ticket for the end of April – the weekend of the Royal Wedding between William and Kate. Needless to say, every flight into London was full, but being a frequent flyer, Craig spoke to a contact at the airport and told her, 'You've got to get me to the UK so that I can pray for a woman with cancer!' That airport employee managed to do as he asked – we don't question how!

His visit prompted mixed emotions in my family. People were just coming to terms with the idea that I was going to die and were understandably worried about me. 'Should Liz really be so expectant for a miracle? Supposing she isn't healed? How would she cope with the disappointment if nothing happened?' I told a few close friends at the Martlets that Craig was coming and Gordon was very enthusiastic about his visit. His faith was rising and so was mine. 'I think God is going to do something,' he said and I had a strong sense that he was right. When the women in the Monday evening prayer group heard the news about Craig they were very excited.

On 29 April I remember watching the Royal Wedding on TV in the lounge with Mum. Understandably, my heart wasn't so much on the celebrations but on something even more exciting. 'Craig must be in the country now,' I kept thinking. 'He'll have landed. He'll be on his way to stay a night with a couple of friends near Lindfield.' What amazed me was how 'local' it all was. We'd been prepared to drive anywhere in the UK where God was on the move, and here was Craig on the doorstep, only about twenty minutes from Sue's house in Hassocks.

The following morning Sue picked me up, then Craig, and drove us back to her home where he was due to stay for the remaining three nights. The ladies' prayer group joined us there, full of faith and expectation for what God was going to do. We met three times over the weekend and on each one we spent time worshipping and thanking God before we prayed – not just for me, but for one another too. Actually, we weren't there just for my sake, we were all very keen to learn from him.

During his time with us Craig gave us his definition of faith from Hebrews 11:1: 'the favourable expectation of things not yet seen'. He also commented on Psalm 50:23: *'The one who sacrifices thank offerings honours me, and I will show him the salvation of God'*. He pointed out that the Greek word for thank offering actually refers to giving thanks for something that's yet to happen. In other words, it's a pure act of faith which honours God and prompts his intervention. Unbeknown to Craig, this was reinforcing what I'd already read in Dodie Osteen's book.

On the first occasion, Craig anointed my forehead with oil before he and others gently laid their hands on me and prayed for my healing. He kept reminding us that he couldn't heal anyone; that was God's remit – and God seemed to be right there with us – he was almost touchable. We sensed that anything could happen! After a while we chilled out and drank coffee and chatted together. Craig was concerned that I might be quite tired and he was right. I disappeared upstairs and lay down for a rest. From that time onwards I never again needed daytime bedrest because of the illness. When I returned, Sue (who'd been a hospice nurse) was struck by the significant change in my countenance. 'Your face is no longer grey,' she said, 'it's pink.' And later she commented that I wasn't nearly as breathless as before.

Tracy was certainly healed. She'd arrived at this first session with her arm in a sling, having recently suffered a badly dislocated shoulder. She was in considerable pain and immediately Craig saw her he nicknamed her 'Broken wing' and prayed for her.

We didn't keep what we were doing from our church leaders. Far from it. They were very happy for Craig to pray for me and one of them, Dave Fellingham, joined us on our second time together. Craig prayed again for me and sensed that I was being held back by things that had happened in my distant family line. He directed me to renounce them. Sue and I spent some time getting to know Craig a bit better. We discovered that his wife, Jenni, prays whenever he engages in ministry. I once saw him on the phone to her, updating her on what was happening. He knew that she'd be praying behind the scenes, even if she had to get up in the early hours of the morning.

On the Sunday morning Craig preached at The Point church in Burgess Hill. I wasn't breathless and drove Mum to the church building. At the end of the service he prayed for me, and many others. I discovered that he never turned anyone away who wanted prayer. That evening he preached at St Andrew's Church, Burgess Hill and Tracy told everyone how God had healed her shoulder and raised her arm with ease. The place was packed with people from churches across the region.

Monday morning arrived. Having prayed for me on Saturday morning, on Sunday afternoon and at both church services, Craig announced, 'I don't think we need to pray for you again. What would you like to do today? Let's go and visit a couple I know who live near Storrington.' Craig, Sue and I drove over for afternoon tea. While we were there one of the wife's friends heard that Craig was in town and called in. Craig prayed for her and Sue and I realised that we were getting a training session on how to pray for people to be healed.

The sale of my house was completed on 3 May – Craig's last day in the UK. I drove alone to my home and walked from room to room, thanking God for the 19 years of ownership and drove to the estate agent to drop off the keys. Then it was back to Mum's house, my now official residence. Sue drove Craig over to see Mum and me and sat with us drinking tea and chatting. He prayed for Mum. Then he left with Sue and me in my car which, by then, I was driving short distances. We had a rushed lunch with the couple in Storrington and then picked up a woman who wanted to come with us to meet her friend who was very sick. She'd arranged a rendezvous with this friend in Costa Coffee at Heathrow Airport.

I have a car with a manual gearbox. For reasons that I don't fully understand, I never used the fifth gear. It may have been that I tried it one day, got in a pickle and lost the confidence to try again. Well, as we speeded on the motorway towards the airport Craig commented on this peculiarity and then proceeded to educate me. I thought that this was quite a novel event – Craig was ending a powerful visit to the UK teaching me how to drive! Now whenever I shift up to fifth gear I thank God for Craig and bless him.

We arrived at Terminal 1 at about 4:00pm and had about an hour before Craig's flight. At Costa Coffee we met the woman who had cancer together with her partner who'd come to give her moral support. Not wanting to intrude on their conversation, Sue, the woman's friend and I sat slightly apart from the other three. But we saw him pray for the sick woman and heard him relate his miraculous story. After he'd explained the gospel message he asked them if there was any reason why they shouldn't accept Christ there and then. Both of them immediately gave their lives to Jesus. (I subsequently heard that the woman's health improved and that she and her partner got married.) Ten minutes later Sue and I were waving Craig through the departure gate and were headed for home.

The 'driving lesson on the motorway' incident stayed in my mind because it brought back to me the strong sense of future that I'd had on the return journey from Sarah's wedding. For a long time I'd been going along in fourth gear, frightened to move up. Craig's visit somehow marked the turning point. The road was opening up for me and I was going to need fifth gear in the days that lay ahead.

CHAPTER 11

YELLOW BRICK ROAD

Some people who are involved in the healing ministry would now be telling me to believe God for a miracle and immediately come off all my medication. But in some cases, healing is a process. I appreciated Craig's wisdom. He released me from any sense of guilt for not throwing all my pills down the toilet, but gave space for the miracle to happen. 'Don't stop the medication or the counselling,' he said, 'and keep going to the Martlets. Let's see what God does.' My walk along God's highway was going to be step by step, not a 100 metre dash. Walking into healing suddenly became my chief objective.

Sometime after Craig had returned to New Zealand I noticed a really nice pair of suede shoes on eBay and bought them. To an onlooker it might have been puzzling that I was buying footwear when I had a death sentence over me, but it was a pure act of faith. I was telling God: 'I believe that I'll be wearing these in the years that lie ahead'. I bought them simply because I liked the colour: red. And at the time it never occurred to me that in the Wizard of Oz Dorothy walked along a yellow brick road wearing ruby shoes. How remarkable is that? I even had the footwear for God's highway!

Craig had given the prayer group his definition of faith: 'the favourable expectation of things not yet seen'. I started stepping out on his words. Up until then I'd virtually let everything go in regard to my personal appearance and desires. There didn't seem to be much point in spending anything on myself, seeing as I'd soon be dead. However, within a week

71

of Craig's leaving I began living as if I were going to survive. I wore night clothes only at night and got dressed for each day. I was driving everywhere and was occasionally riding my bicycle round Hove Recreation Ground, along the very same route that my Mum and I had taken when I first got my cancer diagnosis. On 12 May I went to the hairdresser's for a cut with highlights and in the following week I drove Sue into Brighton because I wanted to buy her a birthday present. We walked around busy shops, enjoyed coffee together and just had fun doing normal things. Several hours later we returned home. Sue's birthday was on 21 May and in the few days beforehand I put my PA skills into play and organised a meal for about twenty members of the family. It was bizarre. At Sarah's wedding my relatives were tearfully expecting never to see me again and within six weeks I was organising a celebration for them!

At the end of May I went with Mum and Sue to one of the open houses connected with the Brighton Festival. While we were there I noticed a watercolour print by a local artist and really liked it. The picture depicted a row of beach huts on the Hove seafront. I love walking by the sea and it reminded me of a time when I was interested in photography and tried to take photos of the same beach huts myself – with mixed results! I bought the print. What I was saying was, 'I'm putting faith into action and investing in the future.'

The Monday evening prayer group continued meeting – we weren't going to disband and stop interceding just because Craig was no longer around. In fact, everyone was just as excited and fervent about praying as they always had been. And emails were flying backwards and forwards between us. I was updating my friends on what was happening to me and they were replying with encouraging Bible verses and exhortations to everybody to keep crying out to God for my complete healing.

I couldn't deny it: the signs were encouraging. As each week went by I noticed that my health was improving. I was no longer nauseous; all the puffiness in my face had disappeared; I wasn't getting breathless; my night sweats ceased; the gurgling stopped and my hands were no longer tingling. My appetite was returning and I was actually beginning to enjoy my food. I was soon lying flat on my bed – for the first time since I'd had the stent fitted the previous October. It was incredible. For about seven months my bedhead had been at a 50 degree angle and I lived with the fear that if I lay flat, I'd aspirate my stomach contents. Now I was lying down properly, my sleep pattern improved drastically. I can't say what a relief that was!

Indeed I was feeling so much better that I suggested to the Martlets' staff that I began withdrawing from my medication. 'We wouldn't advise that, Liz,' they said. We'd expect to increase your medication in the coming weeks'. When I heard this I approached my GP and asked him if I could reduce the slow release morphine and anti-depressants very very gradually. He agreed to this. At the time I was on eighty milligrams of slow release morphine a day, plus ten milligrams of liquid morphine every six hours for the breakthrough pain (pain that occurs in cancer patients between regular painkillers). And I was on 20 milligrams of anti-depressants.

As people at the Martlets saw me holding my own, they started asking questions: 'What's going on, Liz? What's happened to you?' As a result I had a few opportunities to share about God's goodness and occasionally to pray for individuals. What astounded them was my response to a Martlets fundraising activity organised for mid-June. Tracy, the friend whose shoulder was healed, was doing the annual thirteen mile Midnight Walk around Brighton and Hove and invited me to join her for some of it. So instead of dying, I decided to accompany her! I completed about four miles (seven kilometres) of the course and although we were going at quite a pace, I didn't feel tired at all. Tracy and I raised over £400 between us.

My brother-in-law, Mike bought tickets for my third Elton John concert. So on 26 June, Sue, Mike, Mum and I walked to the Sussex County Cricket Ground – it took us about fifteen minutes. The return journey was uphill, but I had no sign of breathlessness and treated everyone to an ice cream. I couldn't get over the fact that I'd just been sitting listening to one of my favourite artists when a few months before I'd been within a whisker of death. God was so good. At the beginning of July I went to my first church service in ages and sat near the back with Rosey. We didn't stay for long at the end of the meeting. It was one thing to be among a crowd at a concert but quite another to have to field questions from church members. They were thrilled, even shocked to see me but I was emotionally overwhelmed, so we slipped away quietly.

When my oncologist had first diagnosed my cancer as terminal, he suggested that I might live until December at the very outside. But I got the impression that I was expected to die by the summer. The patients who'd started attending the Martlets when I did had been given the same kind of prognosis, which was why I lost a number of friends over the next few months.

Dr Robinson's comment, 'You might live until December' was said kindly, to give me hope, but his words somehow hung over me and I was plagued by the thought. 'Will I get past this milestone...and that one?' It was a battle on all fronts: physically, emotionally and spiritually. Reducing my medication was a challenge because I'd been taking it for so long and by the middle of the month I was feeling unwell, lightheaded, weak and tight-chested and was filled with a sense of doom. This reaction didn't nullify God's healing, it was actually a result of my being anaemic and was rectified by a course of iron tablets.

Having said that, I was still reluctant to rest – everything had always been so hard-fought and I thought, 'If I stop I'll deteriorate.' I couldn't help wondering, 'Will I really get past Christmas? Maybe Dr Robinson was right after all'. I told my praying friends what was happening and they were immediately on my case, meeting up with me, sending me encouraging emails and texts and bolstering my faith with words of Scripture and pictures that God had given them. What a team!

By the end of August I'd reduced the slow release morphine

to fifty milligrams a day and had halved my anti-depressants. I still had some periods of back pain but the extreme tiredness was lifting. I was conscious that sometimes food seemed to be sticking briefly in the stent, but I had a new assurance that God would continue to show me the way through.

The Martlets had given me confidence, nevertheless, I felt that I needed to break free of 'patient mode' and live as though I were normal. 'I don't need to be picked up by the minibus now.' I told them, 'I'm going to drive in.' They were astonished at the idea.

On 1 September I wrote to my praying friends: 'The Martlets was mixed on Tuesday. My two best remaining friends are not doing well. I've also heard that one of our number has died and another three regulars have been hospitalised and are on the same ward at the Sussex County! I feel that God is starting to call me out of the Martlets. I do not see myself attending at all by the end of the year – looking to him for wisdom and strategy. Praise God for all he is doing. And thank you all for walking this path with me.'

In the early morning of Tuesday 6 September one of my best friends died and another wasn't at the day centre. I understood that the MacMillan nurses were going to visit her so on 8 September I wrote a short message telling her that Jesus cared for her and posted it through her front door. I never saw her again. Later that same day Mum tripped on the kerb getting into the car, fell over and was rushed to A&E where we spent the next eleven hours. She'd seriously injured herself, fracturing her right shoulder in four places and returned home in considerable pain. She was told that she'd need a major operation to rectify the problem.

Initially Mum was at home in bed drugged up to the eyeballs because of the pain. Indeed, her medication was so strong that she really couldn't function properly, so we had a succession of nurses and carers from the Hospital Trust 'Rapid Response Team' coming in to help me look after her. Suddenly all my focus had been totally redirected. I was no longer thinking about my own recovery, but about Mum's wellbeing. After two weeks of frantic activity and no news on the operation, I decided that a nursing home might be the best option in the short term. While I spent a lot of time with Mum, the intensity of the situation lessened. She had the operation at the end of September and was then admitted to another nursing home for rehabilitation. She stayed there until 19 December.

One morning I'd just arrived at the nursing home to see Mum when my mobile phone rang. The woman on the other end of the line told me that she was calling from my mobile provider. 'You're on a Pay As You Go tariff,' she said, 'and have a dongle with us. Can we interest you in a contract? We can do you a really good deal for the next twenty-four months.' I was caught off guard but was also thinking, 'This is a real challenge. Do I really believe that I'll be alive in the next two years?' So making a very deliberate choice I said to her, 'Yes, I'll take it'.

Meanwhile, I was still attending the Martlets. In fact, I was on the cusp of telling the staff that I was going to cut down my Tuesday visits to two a month and then one. But God intervened and chose my final date for me. I received a letter from the Martlets dated 18 October telling me that although the hospice would continue to function, the day centre would be closing down on 26 October. I went there for the last time on the day before it closed. There were so many vehicles in the car park that I had to leave the car round the corner and walk. It was such a sad occasion, for staff and patients alike. The day centre had been a lifeline for so many and it was heart-wrenching to part from all my friends. At the end of the afternoon Gordon handed me a watercolour of a country scene that he'd painted. 'This is for you,' he said. 'I've called it, *A Different Picture*. What God has for you is completely different.' I interpreted his words to mean that my future was secure. He came out with me and helped me to put my belongings in the car. Then he walked away. I watched him, hoping that he'd look back and wave. But he simply turned the corner and was gone.

CHAPTER 12

UNCHARTED TERRITORY

My days at the Martlets may have ended, but after Mum's fall I certainly hit the ground running. Mum didn't much like the food at the nursing home, so at around 12:30pm every day I picked her up, drove her home and gave her lunch. She'd then spend about five hours with me before I took her back for the night. It was full on. God was clearly forcing me out of patient mode and tipping me into a new reality. As Mum recovered from her operation it became clear that she'd never live independently again. She wouldn't be able to use the bathroom as she had before, so suddenly I was required to plan and co-ordinate a major bathroom refit. The plumbers started work in early November and spent several weeks at the house.

Up until this time I'd managed to make significant reductions in my medication. But in November I was in the middle of a trauma. Christmas was looming; I was struggling to face the physical demands of each day. And there was always the mental battle, that tempting whisper in the night, 'The cancer hasn't gone; you're going to die. There's no way you'll make it into 2012.' I'd lie in bed declaring verses of Scripture, determined not to let go of God's promises. But it was still hard to stand against the devastating prognosis from the oncologist, let alone cope with Mum's poor health and major home improvements. I increased my morphine and anti-depressants just for one month.

In early December, I succumbed to a flu-type bug and began

suffering from a lot of sickness. The plumbers were very sympathetic. They knew that Mum was unwell but were also aware of my terminal diagnosis and that I'd been attending the Martlets. So when they saw me vomiting I think that they interpreted my sickness as a kind of death knell! One of them, Gary, used to bring me a hot water bottle (a present he had bought as my old one was somewhere in a packing box) and a cup of tea. It was a rather unusual scenario really. Now I wasn't under the care of the Martlets but of the plumbers!

Mum returned home a week before Christmas, by which time we'd arranged some additional caring support for an hour every morning. For me it was a rude awakening because there was no respite. God wasn't saying, 'You're getting better, Liz and things will be great from here on.' Certainly my health was improving, but I was facing the demands of being a full time carer for my Mum, who was now dependent on me to do everything for her. I accepted God's path for me but it was physically and emotionally draining. We celebrated Christmas at Jane's house but Mum and I were at home on 31 December. New Year's Eve was never a particularly big event in our family and this year was no exception. However, on this occasion I remember standing in my bedroom looking out of the window at the night sky and thanking God that he'd allowed me to step into 2012.

I began reading a book called *Heaven* by Randy Alcorn (Tyndale House, 2004) and it had a dramatic effect on my life. Up to this point I'd really been quite fearful of death, but Randy's words really stirred me and gave me a genuine excitement about the prospect of eternity with Jesus. Maybe it was ironic that at the same time as I was receiving this encouragement, I was getting better! My life was settling into a kind of normality. I was eating well and slowly weaning myself off the painkillers and anti-depressants. Seeing how much better I was, the members of the weekly Monday night prayer group agreed that we could now meet every two weeks.

On 31 January I had a blood test and on 6 February I saw the consultant at the Martlets for the results. I sat down with her and she smiled and got out the relevant paperwork which she'd covered in yellow highlighter. 'The blood test is excellent,' she said. 'You're not anaemic, your liver function is good, the red and white cell count is fine and, at 15.2, you've probably got one of the highest haemoglobin levels in the whole city!' Then, with a laugh of amazement she added, 'Basically you can go out and buy your Easter eggs. You've got a future.' The following month the senior nurse of the Macmillan Community Team told me that my file was being moved to the temporary discharge cabinet at the Martlets.

The 8 March marked my forty-fifth birthday. I'll never forget how I celebrated: I got on my bed and bounced forty-five times on it! I don't suppose that the bed will forget that day either.

During the spring I went to see my GP every two or three months mainly to discuss Mum's medication, but also to update him on how I was managing to wean myself off my prescription drugs. He was astonished at my progress. One day my nephew, James and I were sitting in the car. As I drove I turned to him and asked, 'What would you say if God had healed me?' He looked at me and replied, 'I'd say that he was very kind.'

On 20 April Smudge arrived. He was a black and white kitten and Mum really enjoyed him. I'd always wanted a kitten and before I was ill I was planning to get one – so he somehow completed the family. His addition to the family was another affirmation to God and to myself, namely, 'I believe that I'm going to be around to look after this little 'furball' in the future.'

In May Mum was experiencing a few intermittent digestive issues so the GP referred her to the Sussex County Hospital. In his referral letter to the Digestive Diseases Department he mentioned that her daughter had a history of oesophageal cancer. While we were there the Consultant referred to the GP's letter and assumed that I couldn't possibly be the daughter mentioned in it. When I told him, 'Yes, that's me,' he replied, 'Well you don't look like you've got cancer to me.' At this point a nurse who was in the room piped up, 'I thought I recognised you. I was on the team when you had one of your endoscopies.' When I told the doctor that people had prayed for me he said, 'Have you always been a Christian or are you born again?!' He then told me how well I was looking, shook my hand (twice actually) and said, 'You need to book an appointment to visit my colleagues because they'll be shocked to see you looking like this.'

By June Mum was regaining some mobility and I was ferrying her back and forth to her weekly Bridge Club and to various doctor's appointments. I also returned to the YMCA to visit the colleagues whom I hadn't seen for two years. Amazingly, I was still employed by the YMCA and with the improvement in my health, I began working there in a voluntary capacity for two hours a week, hoping that one day I might even be able to return permanently. However, in August it became apparent that with Mum's needs, I'd never be in a position to return to do that, so I accepted a redundancy package and changed my profession to Mum's full-time carer. After all that she'd done for me, it was the least I could do for her.

As I withdrew from the morphine my body protested hard. It was with some relief that Craig returned the same month for a few days' ministry in the UK. He anointed me with oil and told me that he thought that I was experiencing phantom pain. My brain was telling my nerve endings that I was in pain because my body didn't want me to withdraw from the morphine. He broke the influence of the drug over me and within a short time I was down to ten milligrams of slow release morphine a day. On 4 September I was drug free.

In November I developed a persistent cough which lasted for a few weeks. I went to my GP who rapidly referred me to the Hove Polyclinic for a chest X-ray mentioning my medical history to them. They gave me the X-ray and told me that they'd contact my doctor if there was a problem. I heard nothing. Naturally, I wanted to know the results, so I made an appointment to see my GP on 4 December. 'There's nothing to report,' he told me. 'The X-ray is normal.' At this point I said to him, 'Do you think it's time that I went back to the hospital? Could you refer me to Dr Robinson?' He agreed that this was a good idea and promised to write a letter to him. Then he commented on how well I looked, threw his hands in the air and with an air of happy bewilderment declared, 'I don't know what's going on. This is uncharted territory.'

CHAPTER 13

THOUGH YOU SEARCH

Mum was just about walking with two sticks when disaster struck. Early on the morning of 8 December I was woken up by the sound of an almighty crash coming from her bedroom. Apparently she'd had a dream, maybe a flashback, in which she imagined that I was dying. In her confusion, she'd darted out of bed to help me but had stumbled and fallen against the door. I forced my way into her room and phoned for an ambulance. When the paramedics arrived they suspected (correctly) that she'd broken her hip and whisked her off to hospital. She had a hip replacement the next day, remained in hospital for the next two weeks and was then transferred to Craven Vale, an excellent Council-run rehabilitation centre where she could receive physiotherapy. She loved Craven Vale and I was happy that she was safe and content. I'd visit her daily and she'd tell me how great the food was there. She'd enjoyed succulent roast pork with crackling when I'd had mere beans on toast! She returned home on 6 January but was never able to regain her former mobility.

On 14 February 2013 Sue accompanied me to the Sussex Cancer Centre for my referral appointment with Dr Robinson. As we walked into his office he stood, stretched out his hand to shake mine and looked at me, half smiling, half quizzical. The last time he'd seen me he'd advised me to put my affairs in order. 'I don't do re-referrals, Liz' he said! 'What are your symptoms? How's your swallow? Are you in any pain?' 'No symptoms,' I replied. 'No pain. And I'm caring for Mum now!'

He gave me a quick physical examination and said that he'd book me in for another CT scan. Then he wrote to my GP in a letter which was typed on 26 February:

'Many thanks for re-referring this delightful lady who, as you describe, was diagnosed with advanced oesophageal cancer with lung metastases just over 2 years ago. She really has done extraordinarily well and if anything has been improving recently with an increase in appetite, swallowing and weight.

'Physical examination was unremarkable and certainly I think it would be appropriate to re-evaluate her stage of disease currently and I have booked her for a repeat CT scan. I will ask for her case to be discussed at our local multidisciplinary meeting and contact her with the results of the scan when it is available.'

I had the CT scan of my thorax and abdomen on 11 March and Dr Robinson phoned me on the 27th. At the time I was in Sainsbury's supermarket. 'I've got news for you,' he said. 'Is it good news?' I asked. He continued, 'It's excellent news. The CT scan shows no evidence of disease either in the oesophagus or in the lung. But we saw lung lesions before and we want to know what they were. We'd like to recommend some further tests with a repeat endoscopy and a PET CT scan to establish the state of the cancer currently in the oesophagus and whether there's any disease further afield. There's one anomaly: we can't see the stent, which we suspect has migrated to your stomach.'

I was elated. Immediately I phoned both Sue and Jane and they were ecstatic and very emotional. The supermarket security camera tapes must have made for some interesting viewing; you can almost hear the comments: 'What's up with that woman in the pickle aisle? She hasn't moved for ages. Something's definitely got her animated.'

On 12 April I presented myself at the Hove Polyclinic. I lay down on the couch and the staff took the X-ray. Then there was a bit of a commotion in the corner of the room. A young radiologist came over to me and said, 'It was oesophageal cancer that you had, wasn't it?' 'Yes,' I replied. 'Well,' he went on, 'we can't see the stent and need to clarify with the Sussex County that this is what we're looking for. We don't want to look foolish if we're not doing this right.' As I lay there waiting for him to return I remembered God's words from Isaiah 41: *'Though you search for your enemies, you will not find them. Those who wage war against you will be as nothing at all.'*

Having made his phone call the young man returned to me and continued, 'The hospital staff want us to take a second X-ray, higher up, to make sure that there's no mistake; so in effect you'll have had your whole body X-rayed!' They did the second image and afterwards as I came out of the changing cubicle he said, 'Where's the stent gone? Surely people don't pass stents, do they?' As I walked by reception on my way out I saw the staff pouring over the X-rays, looking puzzled. Not only had the cancer gone; the metal stent had disappeared as well.

People of a scientific persuasion are often keen to explain anomalies, which is probably why my body was being subjected to such scrutiny. There had to be a logical explanation. Maybe the cancer had spread somewhere else. Maybe the ten centimetre stent had passed through my entire digestive system without my noticing it! Two years previously, when the doctors first began to suspect that something was seriously wrong with me, they acted very fast. Naturally, they didn't want to waste time when they could be addressing my illness. Now everything seemed to be equally as swift, but the motivation was different. There had to be a reason why a terminal cancer patient was now completely well and they were going to find it.

I had the PET scan of my whole body on 18 April and the endoscopy just five days later. The search for an answer meant that I was required to undergo some invasive treatments. It was another 'garden hose down the throat' experience – not an event that I ever enjoyed much! The endoscopy tube was inserted right down into my stomach as far as my duodenum and biopsies were taken. Later the nurse practitioner on duty told me that there was a minor stricture at the lower end of my oesophagus where the tumour had once been. She could see no evidence of cancer now.

When I returned to the hospital with Sue on 9 May to

discuss the results of the tests, I found that Dr Robinson was sick and that we'd be seeing his colleague, Dr Green instead. Dr Green told us that the team was amazed at my story. The PET scan was clear; the gastroscopy biopsies were clear; there was no cancer and no stent. He informed us that at the multidisciplinary meeting the team had engaged in a long discussion about me. How could I be well when I'd had no additional medical treatment? They came up with several suggestions:

1. The original diagnosis was wrong – but they had numerous test results (CT, endoscopic) and biopsy evidence that it was correct.
2. The chemotherapy had started to take effect in the months after my terminal diagnosis – but this wasn't a plausible possibility.
3. Because I was a younger person my immune system had suddenly kicked in and dealt with the cancer – but this was also highly unlikely, and the chemotherapy would have greatly weakened my immune system anyway.

The medics couldn't account for my recovery, but because they wanted to make sure that the tests were totally comprehensive, they still wanted one final endoscopy. This would include biopsies from even deeper in my oesophageal wall to double check that everything really was OK.

Initially I flinched at the idea, but when I learnt that the request had come from Mr Hale, the consultant surgeon who'd initially broken the news that I had cancer to me, I relented. 'If Mr Hale wants me to go through this again, I'll do it,' I said. 'But it will be the last one. I don't want any more tubes down my throat.' Before I left his consulting room Dr Green said, 'Your case is rare. You're weird! I know you're a woman of faith, so if you say that God has healed you, then who am I to argue with that?'

Immediately Sue and I got outside the Cancer Centre we looked at one another and were so excited that, like children, we jumped up and down for sheer joy. The team had simply endorsed what we already knew and we were going to have our mini-celebration no matter what!

The final endoscopy was performed by a consultant on 3 June. Afterwards he came into the recovery room to see me and to say that Dr Robinson had done a good job. He was under the impression that I'd had all kinds of recent therapies and was baffled by my comment that the only treatment I'd received since January 2011 was persevering prayer. It came as no surprise to me when, weeks later, the deep biopsies were confirmed as all clear.

I had a hard job trying to convince government authorities that I was well and no longer needed my benefits. I sent off a letter from Dr Robinson, and filled in various forms, only to have the paperwork questioned and sent back with the comment, 'We can't do this until we have a report from your GP.' With some persuasion, they finally agreed to cease paying me.

So far, the summer had been wet and windy, but on Saturday 6 July, it changed and the sun appeared. I'd arranged for people to gather to celebrate my healing. Outside Mum's house the family put up a big arrow which read, 'The party's here.' It pointed in the direction of the back garden where we'd erected a gazebo and hung lots of bunting. There was food and drink and the centrepiece was a large cake bearing the words: *To God be the glory great things he has done.*

Our guests arrived between 12:00 and 3:00 – all ninety of them! They were the people who'd played some part in my journey: Christians, unbelievers, family members, friends, neighbours, carers, tradesmen, ex-colleagues from the YMCA and friends from the Martlets. Gordon came, and I reminded him of the painting *A Different Picture* that he'd given me almost two years previously.

Steve gave a superb speech and asked everyone to raise their glasses to the Lord, or to me if they didn't believe in God. I wasn't expecting to respond so when I saw the sea of faces looking in my direction, I was completely lost for words. I said something like, 'This could have been a wake, but instead it's a celebration' and then stopped. I couldn't say any more because I was so choked with emotion. But maybe it had already been said. Everyone knew how thankful I was to them for all the support they'd given me. And how could I ever find the words to express my utter amazement and deep gratitude at the way that God had chosen to work? So I just left it to the celebration cake to declare his greatness for me.

CHAPTER 14

SKYLINE PIGEON

Several years before my cancer diagnosis, Mike, my brother-in-law, decided that for his fiftieth birthday he wanted to have an Elton John themed party and I decided to dress up as the Skyline Pigeon. I spent ages making the costume and attaching the different coloured feathers. The night before the party I was up until the early hours finishing it off. I also made a special bespoke birthday card with a pigeon on it with the words of the song inside:

> Turn me loose from your hands
> Let me fly to distant lands
> Over green fields, trees and mountains
> Flowers and forest fountains
> Home along the lanes of the skyway
>
> For this dark and lonely room
> Projects a shadow cast in gloom
> And my eyes are mirrors
> Of the world outside
> Thinking of the way
> That the wind can turn the tide
> And these shadows turn
> From purple into grey
>
> For just a Skyline Pigeon
> Dreaming of the open

Waiting for the day
He can spread his wings
And fly away again
Fly away skyline pigeon fly
Towards the dreams
You've left so very far behind

Just let me wake up in the morning
To the smell of new mown hay
To laugh and cry, to live and die
In the brightness of my day

I want to hear the pealing bells
Of distant churches sing
But most of all please free me
From this aching metal ring
And open out this cage towards the sun

Written by Bernie Taupin

According to Wikipedia the ballad was supposed to represent someone who wanted to be released from a broken marriage and set free to pursue new dreams and ambitions. But for me, at the time of greatest battle against terminal cancer and deep depression, the last twenty words touched me far deeper than that: *But most of all please free me from this aching metal ring and open out this cage towards the sun.* The aching metal ring wasn't a band around my wedding finger; it was the stent inside my oesophagus which was then causing me great distress, and from which I longed to be free.

Early one morning in mid-July 2013 I woke up to the sound of a huge commotion downstairs and headed off to see what was happening. My bleary eyes were met with a strange sight: one cat and one bird – both in Mum's kitchen. Smudge had somehow hit the jackpot! He'd managed to catch a large pigeon and drag it into the house through the cat flap. Unfortunately, once he'd released his grip slightly, the bird had got away from him. Both were now panicked: Smudge was backed up against a wall, unable to cope with the enormity of his prize and the pigeon was flapping crazily against the kitchen window trying to get out. There were downy feathers everywhere.

When I arrived the pigeon calmed down, sat and looked at me. He seemed healthy enough. His wings were obviously working fine and I couldn't see any wounds. As the early morning rays shone through the window, they picked out a lovely range of colours all down his front. I was struck by their beauty.

I found the key, unlocked and opened the window and he just sat there looking at me. I reached over the sink and he let me cradle him in my hands. Then I put my arms through the window and, with a slight upward movement, gently let him go. He swooped down over the lawn and then soared upward towards the skyline. As that happened God spoke to me: 'This is what I've done for you, Liz. I've opened the cage and turned you loose. You're free.'

When I saw Dr Robinson in May 2014 he smiled, confirmed that I was well, shook my hand and said, 'Come and brighten up my day in a year's time.' I did just that! In May 2015 I saw him again and promised to give him a copy of my book. 'You'll have it in your hand by the time I next see you,' I told him. And I got the impression that he made a final appointment for me just to ensure that I kept my word to him!

My nephew, James was absolutely right when he told me that if I was healed, he'd consider God 'very kind'. There are some who might dispute this. When one man heard my story he commented: 'How could a good God allow you to go through such suffering, take you to the edge and create such devastation among your family members?' I don't know the answer, nor can I explain why God chose to send someone from the other side of the world to seal my healing.

I often find myself reflecting on God's extravagant grace to me. Not only did he fully restore me physically, but mentally and emotionally too. I'm a totally different person from the one that I once was. I don't know what God has in store for me, but I know he's good, I believe I've been saved for a purpose and I am in his hands. I have a future. I'm looking out of another window, waiting for the day when he allows me to spread my wings even more and fly towards new dreams and a new skyline.

TRIBUTE

An orchestra, a clock, a sports' team – when their parts work well together, there's harmony, even beauty. It's no wonder that God refers to his church as a body. His people are interconnected and when they work together towards a common goal their unity results in his blessing (Psalm 133).

This book could have ended with Chapter 14 but I couldn't 'sign off' without a final tribute to the Monday night prayer group because I doubt that I'd have coped with my ordeal if it hadn't been for them. The support that they gave me was superb, and I'll never forget their outstanding commitment to me.

Tracy was the group orchestrator. She was at a dinner party when someone told her that I had oesophageal cancer. On the day I had my terminal diagnosis, she came round to Mum's house and sat and cried with me. Later she sensed that God was directing her to gather a small group of faith-filled people to pray regularly for me, and the team of six was established.

The group dynamic was interesting. Jesus chose twelve disciples whom few others would have put together. The same thing happened in my case. Initially, some of the team were almost strangers to me and to one another too. They were all busy people, from different walks of life and with a wide range of gifts and abilities. But the one thing that they all had in common was this: they wanted to be involved with Someone whom Tracy said, 'could make the impossible possible and bring the supernatural into the natural realm'.

Little did we know then how much God would teach us about interacting with him and honouring one another to accomplish something totally magnificent.

As I grew weaker and weaker, some well-meaning Christians thought that it was time to stop praying for my healing and focus on a good death. But these women would have none of it. They were outraged at the idea that cancer should be allowed to take me and tenaciously fought for my healing. Certainly, they all had periodic doubts about my survival, but they simply refused to let go, convinced that persevering prayer was a big key to winning the battle.

While the Martlets was a physical, emotional and social oasis, the Monday night group kept me going emotionally, socially and spiritually. We all looked forward to our meetings and each one was different because the Holy Spirit was leading and teaching us. Sometimes we'd just have fun together and laugh, which was great medicine. But on most occasions we'd engage in a glorious mix of worship, thanksgiving, prayer, Scripture, prophecy, mental 'pictures' and tongues, with some of these aspects more prevalent than others depending on what God was doing among us at the time. And there were instances when the atmosphere was so charged with God's presence that it seemed as though he'd actually walked into the room.

Not only did these friends pray for me on Monday nights, they cried out to God for me on many other occasions. **Irene**, who was also my church counsellor, probably spoke for them all when she commented, 'I remember many days and nights when I felt strong pressure to pray, and many walks on the Downs when I was praying hard in tongues as well as English.' I regularly received emails or text messages giving me verses of Scripture to encourage me. **Claire** seemed to have an uncanny knack of hitting on exactly the right Bible passage, which was often unwittingly endorsed by one of the others. And if I needed emergency prayer support all I had to do was text the word, SWORD to them.

The team supported me in other ways too (as did others outside the group). On several occasions **Valerie** would pop round to lay hands on me and, to coin a phrase, 'soak me in the Holy Spirit'. And **Julie** used her creative skills to make me a mobile. At the end of each string was a delicate butterfly whose wings were a combination of tissue paper and paper printed with Bible verses from Isaiah, notably chapter 41: 'Though you search...' It was exquisite.

Sue, my sister, was the sixth member. Naturally, she was more involved with me than all the others and had immediate access to information about what was going on and through great networking skills was able to make the important connections. She ferried me around, contacted and updated Craig on my condition and joined me in paying a proportion of his return airline ticket.

The group members were prepared to fight for my recovery regardless of how much it cost. It's no wonder that I have a deep affection for them. We had amazing times together and as the weeks passed our faith levels rose and we dared to believe that God could heal me. So when Craig arrived on the scene, the preparation for a miracle had already been done. He just put the final piece into the jigsaw and the picture, *A Different Picture*, was complete.

The team remained together for an eighteen month season. When I was healed it disbanded, although I did still see individuals socially and continued to receive periodic counselling from Irene into early 2014. We parted not only with a cry of victory, but also with a greater sense of awe at what God could accomplish and a deepening awareness of how to tune into the Spirit and pray for his intervention. He led us all in a wonderful, if demanding adventure. And none of us will ever be the same again.

Finally...
If you want to know how much God cares for you, or if you need his intervention in your own life, let me encourage you to seek Jesus. Look for him in books and on the Internet or attend a local Alpha Course and talk to Bible-believing Christians. If you don't belong to a local church, find one where the members know that Jesus works miracles today.